If you want the absolute *easiest* trees, flowers, shrubs, and grass to plant and maintain, **GOLFER'S GUIDE TO GARDENING** is *the* book for you. Look at the Table of Contents and see that what I'm telling you is correct.

You see, I love Gardening—it's my life—but I also enjoy other activities and there didn't seem to be enough time to do both. But, being the kind of person who *likes to have their cake and eat it too*, I've solved that problem.

Because of my study and research, as well as gardening tips from my **KTRH GardenLine** listeners, I decided to write this book especially for golfers or those who have interests other than gardening so you too can do both.

Randy Lemmon

GOLFER'S
GUIDE
to
GARDENING

by

RANDY LEMMON

SWAN PUBLISHING
TEXAS ✦ CALIFORNIA ✦ NEW YORK

Author: Randy Lemmon
Editors: Pete Billac & Pinkney Newton Hartline
Cover Design: Cindy Coker
Layout Designer: Sharon Davis

Copyright @ April 1997 Randy Lemon and Swan Publishing
Library of Congress #97-65259
ISBN #0-943629-28-4

GOLFER'S GUIDE TO GARDENING is available in quantity discounts through SWAN Publishing, 126 Live Oak, Alvin, TX 77511. (281) 388-2547 or Fax (281) 585-3738.

Printed in the United States of America.

DEDICATION

I want to dedicate this book to a group of people—the many dedicated listeners of KTRH GardenLine. Without some consistent cajoling from those callers and listeners who approached me at appearances like the 1996 Home Show, I'm not sure I would have written this book.

Thanks and kudos are also earned by my publisher, Pete Billac, whose unique salesmanship ultimately convinced me to put this book together.

First and foremost, I would like to thank my on-air partner, John Burrow, who worked hard to get me at KTRH. Also, I would like to thank the promotions *gurus* Pam Kehoe and Cindy Bell of KTRH, not only for their friendship, but for their tireless work at promoting GardenLine.

And a special thanks goes out to those extraordinary friends who stuck by me during some seriously tough times, especially Scott "Scooter" Peacock, and Tim Collins, one of the GardenLine producers. But the *biggest* and probably the most important thanks goes to Sherri and Cliff Lee, two of the best friends any person should be allowed to have.

The most serious, loving dedication is to my deceased mother, Phyllis Lemmon-Jones. If she were alive today, I think she would be especially proud of me not only because her son works at arguably the best radio station in Texas, but also because I wrote a book about a subject dear to her heart—gardening. She may not have known it then, but I sure picked up a lot from her as a teenager watching and helping her work feverishly in her gardens she loved so very much. I love you mom.

INTRODUCTION

I absolutely love the beauty and serenity a fine job of landscaping and gardening can bring to a home. I also like the value it adds to the selling price. Usually, when you see a truly great looking yard with flowers and shrubs, the homeowner is retired and spends either lots of time in their garden, or they have two jobs, their regular job and the one working in their garden with little time to do anything else.

As much as gardening is a major part of my life, I don't want to spend *all* of my free time maintaining a garden, and my bet is you don't either! In fact, I would much rather be playing golf. Whatever you like to do with your free time, this book is designed to help provide low-maintenance gardening and landscape tips that will help keep your garden healthy and attractive without you having to spend an inordinate amount of time there to achieve such results, even for an avid gardener. There are lots of tips in this book that will save you even *more* time to stand back and enjoy your accomplishments or, get in another round of golf.

Many of the ideas in this book are ones I try to share with the listeners of my radio program on a daily basis, but because of time constraints, there are really only a few tips we can incorporate each day. This book will help encompass most of the great tips, methods and procedures I've learned over the years from some of the really true experts.

In Texas, we are fortunate to be able to garden pretty much all year round. A friend of mine who moved here from Minnesota 12 years ago still hasn't caught on we can plant *fall colors* in our gardens that will keep looking good until February. He's still programed to giving up on gardening in September and not doing another thing until March.

Gosh! How I love gardening, golf, and Texas. I also truly enjoy my job on GardenLine. Being on the radio a few hours each day six days a week has given me a modicum of recognition. No matter where I am, like the proverbial doctor at a dinner party, when people find out what I do for a living it's only a matter of heartbeats before the questions start. But I don't mind, because I like people, and I enjoy sharing what I've learned with others who care about their gardens.

I've always considered myself a communicator first and a horticulturist somewhere else way down my somewhat limited list of attributes. If you benefit from just a few tips in this book and can learn to have a tremendous landscape without breaking your back, then I think I've done my job.

TABLE OF CONTENTS

Part 1 .... TREES

Ten Best Trees for Texas
Honorable Mention

Part 2 .... ANNUALS

Cool-Colored Annuals
Warm-Colored Annuals
Total Sun-Loving Annuals—Spring
Total Sun-Loving Annuals—Summer
Sun-Loving Annuals—Fall
Mostly Shade-Loving Annuals—Spring & Summer
Mostly Shade-Loving Annuals—Fall
Annuals in Containers

Part 3 .... MULCH

You Can Never Have Enough Mulch
Mulching Material
Mulch Rings Around Trees

Part 4 .... SHRUBS

Full-Sun Plants
Partial-Shade Plants
Total Shade Plants
Other Good Small Shrubs/Groundcovers

Part 5 .... **SOILS**

Planting in Texas Gumbo
Raised Beds
Planting Medium for Indoor Plants

Part 6 .... **NATIVE TEXAS PLANTS**

The NATURAL Garden
Houston Coastal Plains
Piney Woods
Blackland Prairie
Post Oak Plains

Part 7 .... **LAWNS**

Turfgrass   Scalping
Fertilizer   Watering
Ratios/N-P-K   Lawn
When to Fertilize   Diseases
Mowing & Mulching Mowers   Weeds
Thatch   Lawn Reference Guide

Part 8 .... **HOUSE PLANTS**

Drainage & Watering
Potting Medium & Soil Mix
Feeding & Fertilizing

Part 9 .... **INSECTS & DISEASES**

Part 10 .... **CALENDAR CHECKLIST**

GGG Gardening Tips January through December

Trees

One of the most often-asked questions I get on the is, "What is the best shade tree I can plant in this part of the state?" There is not one *silver bullet* answer. Since trees are the largest "plant" in your yard and much of what you plant that is smaller is dictated by the trees, let's start off this first chapter with trees. Here are the parameters of a **ten best list of trees** for this part of the country. This ten best list includes all **deciduous** trees, or, those naturally losing their leaves each winter. I'm choosing those with these most popular attributes:

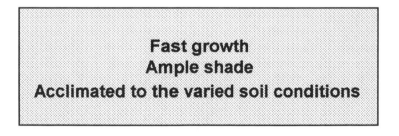

Fast growth
Ample shade
Acclimated to the varied soil conditions

TEN BEST TREES

Green Ash—(*Fraxinus Penssylvanica*)

Despite the popular claim, *Ash is Trash* that only applies to the **Arizona Ash**. I was told long ago the Green Ash was the next best thing to an Arizona Ash when it came to fast growth. The few I planted have borne that out. I took a four foot twig of a green ash, planted it in the caleche soil, (the "Aggie" version or hard, clay soil) of Bryan-College Station, and in three years it was already 16 feet tall.

> **Benefits:** Will top out at 50 to 60 feet. Fast growth. No nasty seed pods like the Arizona Ash. A green leaf *surge* in April for shade protection throughout the summer. One of the last to lose its leaves in the fall.
>
> **Disadvantages:** One of the last to push out new growth in early spring.

White Ash—*(Fraxinus Americana)*

Fastest growing of all the ash trees, but it is not as susceptible to many of the insect and disease pressures. Can grow to as high as 70 feet, which means it doesn't bush out as much as we would like for optimum shade value.

> **Benefits:** Longer lived than the Arizona. Striking fall orange colors.
>
> **Disadvantages:** Very tall. Doesn't give you the dense shade. Often hard to find in local nurseries and must be special ordered.

Nuttall Oak—*(Quercus Nuttallii)*

Similar to the Shumard Red Oak in many ways, but is it's own tree. Has excellent fall color like the Shumard, but with more orange and yellow. (Shumard is more purple/red.) The biggest difference may actually be in the look of the acorn.

They are larger than most oak nuts and they have a unique striped look to them which is also known as a Swamp Red Oak.

Benefits: Fast growth, unique acorns, beautiful fall color of yellow/orange/red. Does very well in clay soil.

Disadvantages: Often mistaken for the Shumard, but not as available.

Overcup Oak—*(Quercus Lyrata)*

Not a *common* tree, but it is gaining in popularity especially among landscape professionals. It is a unique addition to the landscape with its upswept style branches, which translates into the need for little, if any, pruning as the tree ages. While it is considered a fast grower, it will only grow to a maximum of 45 feet.

Benefits: Fast growth. Upswept branches. Landscaper's choice.

Disadvantages: Will max out at 40-45 feet. Not always available except through wholesale growers.

Shumard Red Oak—*(Quercus Shumardii)*

Becoming rapidly popular in the Texas landscape; a fast growing tree that can reach maturity of 60 feet high with a span or 40 feet. It's popularity may be driven not only by its rapid growth but its beautiful reddish/bronze foliage in the fall. This tree is also tolerant of the alkaline soils existing in most parts of Texas. A good tip when picking out Shumard Red Oaks; choose them in the fall to assure getting one which leaves turn bright red. It also needs good drainage for optimum growth.

> **Benefits:** Fast growth, wide span, readily available, beautiful fall colors. Holds leaves until spring, which gives it character.

> **Disadvantages:** One of the last to re-leaf in spring, needs lots of space for 40' spread. Holds brown leaves until spring, which make it look dead to some people.

Mexican Oak—*(Quercus Polymorphas)*

Also becoming more and more popular in Texas landscaping. Another fast-growing tree that reaches 80 feet at maturity with a 40-foot spread. In Mexico they reach 100 feet. Also starts off with maroon colored leaves in early spring.

> **Benefits:** Fast growth, unique colors in fall and spring. Doesn't lose a lot of leaves and seems evergreen in the southern most parts of Texas.

> **Disadvantages:** Questionable hardiness from Central Texas North, although they survived near 0° in Dallas in 1989.

Mexican Sycamore—*(Plantanus Mexicanus)*

I've seen one 10 year-old Mexican Sycamore that was already 60' tall when it was only ten years old and it was still growing. It also provides striking leaves whose undersides looks much like silver leaf maples.

> **Benefits:** Real fast grower. Dense leaves for shade. Beautiful green/silver/white contrast on top and bottom of leaves. Doesn't decline early like American Sycamores. Isn't susceptible to anthracnose.
>
> **Disadvantages:** May still grow too fast like other Sycamores, setting itself up for early decline. Leaf drops are *nasty*, because they are big and bulky like American Sycamores.

Cedar Elm—*(Ulmus Crassifolia)*

An incredibly tough tree, which is what we need in Texas. It has the potential of growing some 75 feet high, but its span only reaches 30-35 feet. This is a *native* Texas tree and one we cannot go wrong with. It is tolerant of many stresses from wet feet, to drought, to urban pollution. And it is more structurally stable than what we think of as standard Elm trees.

> **Benefits:** Drought resistant. *Native* Texas tree. Attractive flaking bark. Fast grower.
>
> **Disadvantages:** Not the most dense leaf from for shade purposes.

Winged Elm *a.k.a.* Corky Winged Elm—*(Imus Alata)*

Another distinctive looking tree because of its corky winged twigs. While it grows fast, it too will only reach a maximum height of 30-40 feet. The best attribute of the Winged Elm is it will still grow rapidly even in some of the poorest soils of this part of the country. However, it will grow even better if you prepare the soils (which we address in Part 5).

> **Benefits**: Unique twigs and bark. Fast growth early in life.

> **Disadvantages:** Never will get real big. Is an elm tree, and they always drop their leaves early.

White Oak—*(Quercus Alba)*

This eventually can be a huge tree; 20-30-year-old White Oaks have been as tall as 90-100 feet with a span of 75-80 feet. However, it is not the fastest growing of the oak family. Still, it beats the Live Oak. An interesting side note on the White Oak: It is prized as wood furniture in many areas, such as the Northeast United States. In fact, the White Oak is the state tree of Connecticut *and* Pennsylvania.

> **Benefits:** Huge growth. Equally huge spread. Beautiful fall purple colors. Prized by wildlife for its acorns.

> **Disadvantages:** Not the fastest growing oak. Must be planted all by itself for its potential growth of 90x75 feet.

Honorable Mention

Bradford Pear *a.k.a.* Ornamental Pear—*(Pyrus Calleryanna*)
Camphor—(*Cinnamomum Lauraccae*)
Drummond Red Maple—*(Acer Rubrom)*

These two trees end up making great shade trees. The Camphor is mostly evergreen, but both are much slower in growth than the above mentioned trees in the ten best list.

There are only two or three **evergreen** trees acceptable for shade value but they all come with their individual draw-backs.

First, the *Pine* tree. While it grows rapidly, it doesn't really provide extensive shade.

Second, *Live Oaks* are one of the best trees we can plant in Houston but take 10 years to give sufficient shade value.

Third, the *Camphor* tree is an excellent evergreen, but a rather slow grower and highly susceptible to freeze damage in these parts.

> No matter which tree/trees you choose to plant, remember the important planting and mulch benefits.

Golf Tip #1:

Good golf ain't cheap!

Part 2

Annuals

For most gardeners, *annuals* mean flowers. Or put another way, they are the ones we plug into a swath of the landscape one or two times a year. But a varied use of annuals is not only aesthetically pleasing, it's one of the *easiest* things we can do to the garden, because they grow so profusely and are relatively easy to care for. Let's talk about annuals.

Most annuals are known by horticulturists to spend their entire growing season producing seeds, which, in our landscape, don't always come back. That's why growing annuals is such an interesting proposition for us in this area. While we want the color a couple of times each year, we don't like the idea of re-investing. Personally, I think it's worth it. And I'm here to tell you that you can spend far less than one hundred dollars each year on a 4x10' square color pocket.

There are three distinctive growing seasons here, which makes annuals the most *flexible* plant material we can work with. Why should we plant annual *X* every February, annual *Y* every June and annual *Z* each November? Because, these are the three best times to cycle out annuals, but do they always have to be in *X-Y-Z* order?

The hardest thing to remember about annuals is how color relationships work. Just because you like this color and that color, doesn't mean they're going to necessarily "work" in your garden. That's because some colors clash and some colors complement each other. If you were to pick out an orange Gerber Daisy, it falls on the color wheel as a *warm* color—which is a *feeling,* not physiological property. A blue/violet flower thus falls on the *cool* feeling color of a color wheel. The reason this is important is because annual colors need be the opposite of the warm or cool color of your house, deck or window sill.

Another way to explain this is if you have a warm colored brick house, a bunch of warm colors like red, yellow and orange make the area even warmer. If you planted violets, blues, yellows or pastels against that warm brick or wood, you now have a considerably *cooler* feeling that will be much more inviting.

Another important consideration is: to the eye, cool colors tend to recede, and warm colors tend to advance; warm colors stand out and shout, helping to bring a distant part of the yard into sharper focus. Generally speaking, cool colors are good for close-up viewing and warm colors are good for dramatic displays further away.

Cool Colors	Warm Colors
Yellow	
Yellow-Green	Dark Yellow;
Green	Yellow-Orange;
Blue-Green	Orange;
Blue	Orange-Red;
Blue-Violet	Red
Violet	Red-Violet
Light yellow	

No matter which colors you choose, mixing whites of whatever species is always a good contrast maker.

The safest way I can recommend working with annuals is to use *color pockets* in a landscape and containerized annual plantings. A color pocket is a tight, small area of intense annual plantings, instead of spreading bedding plants throughout the yard. I'm a big fan of color pockets, because it helps draw particular attention to certain parts of the landscape, and it helps save you loads of money because you need far fewer flats. Plus, color pockets can be a focal point of your landscape and yet another way to alter color schemes throughout the year.

There are literally hundreds upon thousands of annuals that can be grown throughout the U.S. during differing seasons. We, unfortunately, are somewhat limited mainly because of temperature and humidity extremes.

GOLFER'S GUIDE TO GARDENING recommends the following for quite possibly the best annuals for temperature and light conditions listed. That means they don't have to be pampered on a daily basis. Remember, you don't just have to plant Petunias in spring, Vincas in summer and Pansies in the fall. Use these recommendations and impress your family and neighbors with alternatives far beyond what you've thought of before. The following is a list of annuals for the three seasons and whether they do well in sun or shade environments:

Total Sun-Loving Annuals—Spring

Alyssum—Pink; Purple; White
English Daisy—Pink; Purple; White
Geranium—Red; Pink; Purple; White
Larkspur—Orange; Yellow; Violet; Blue; White
Nasturtium—Red; Pink; Orange;Yellow; White
Petunias—Red; Pink; Orange; Yellow; Purple; White; Multis

Phlox—Red; Pink; Purple; White
Primrose—Red; Pink; Yellow; Blue; White
Stock—Red; Pink; Purple; White
Sweet William—Red; Pink; White; Multi-Colored
Verbenas—Red; Pink; Purple; White; Multis
Zinnias—Red; Pink; Orange; Yellow; White; Multi-Colored

Tropicals
Angel's Trumpet—Pink; Orange; Purple; White

Total Sun-Loving Annuals—Summer

Amaranthus—Red; Copper; Green.
Bachelor Buttons—Red; Pink; Orange; Purple; Blue; White.
Dahlia—Red; Pink; Yellow; Purple; White; Multis.
Foxglove—Red; Pink; Yellow; White.
Hollyhocks—Red; Pink; Orange; Yellow; Purple.
Marigolds—Orange; Yellow; White; Multis.
Mexican Heather—Pink; Purple; White.
MossRoss (Portulaca)—Red; Pink; Orange; Yellow; Purple; White; Multis.
Periwinkle (Vincas)—Red; Pink; Purple; White; Multis.
Purslane—Red; Pink; Orange; Yellow; Purple; White; Multis.

Tropicals
Alamanda—Yellow
Bougainvillea—Red; Pink; Orange; Yellow; Purple; White; Multis.
Copper Plant—Yellow; Orange; Copper (Blend)

Mostly Sun-Loving Annuals—Fall

Calendulas—Orange; Yellow; White
Dianthus—Red; Pink; Purple; White; Multis
Dusty Miller—Green; Gray; White (Blend)

Johnny Jump-Ups—Yellow; Blue; Purple
Ornamental Kale—Purple; Green; Gray (Blend)
Ornamental Cabbage—Red; Purple; Green (Blend)
Pansy—(Every Color Imaginable)
Snapdragons—Red; Pink; Orange; Yellow; Purple; White; Multis
Violas—Red; Yellow; Blue; Purple; White

Mostly Shade-Loving Annuals—Spring & Summer

Caladium—(Multi Colored Reds, Purples, Greens,Whites)
Coleus—(Multi Colored Reds, Purples, Pinks, Greens)
Impatiens—Red, Pink, Orange, Purple, White (Some Multis)
New Guinea Impatiens—Red, Pink, Orange, Purple, White (Some Multis)
Wax Begonias—Orange, Pink, Red, White

Tropicals
Croton (Color combos of Yellow, Orange, Red, Pink and Green)

Mostly Shade-Loving Annuals—Fall

Gotcha! THEY DON'T EXIST!

Annuals in Containers

Even if you have lots of trees and a lack of flower beds under those trees, you can still produce annual displays by using containers. In fact, I think annuals and containers were actually made for each other.

Spring pots of Primroses and Pansies can give way to summer flowering Marigolds and Impatiens, and the Golden Mums in the fall can be replaced in mild winter climes with crops of hard annuals like Nasturtium and Pansies.

Another good tip for working with containerized annuals is to purchase *slightly used* and *different sized pots*. And I'm not just talking about *terra cotta* clay pots; use wooden crates, wooden whiskey barrels cut in two, concrete pots, and pots with designs, possibly the newest craze in gardening, like Moons, Stars, Lions, Leprechauns; et.al.

Once you become "good" with annuals and you want more and more plants, and long spans of annuals to line your landscape, you'll learn which ones work best by seeds and at what times of the year to sow those seeds. Be careful though, and try not to be too overtaken with these "wonders of nature" because as you learn to love plants more, it **will** take time away from that golf game.

Mix the annuals listed previously on a yearly basis and again you won't be stuck with the X in spring, the Y in summer and Z in fall. In fact, you'll find some annual species that might even perform better for you than the old standbys of Petunias, Impatience, Pansies and Periwinkles.

Golf Tip #2:

Try to sink *all* your putts if you want to win!

Part 3

Mulch

YOU CAN NEVER HAVE ENOUGH MULCH

"You can never have enough mulch." That's a personal gardening tenet for me and for everyone who aspires to the time-saving tips in GOLFER'S GUIDE TO GARDENING. You simply need to use mulches wherever and whenever possible! Why? Because:

They Reduce Evaporation of Water from the Soil

They Limit Weed Germination

Conserves Moisture (in spring)

Prevents Surface Caking

Conserves Moisture (in summer)

Helps Insulate During Drought Stress

Helps Insulate During Freezes

Conserves Moisture (in winter)

Breaks Down into Useable Organic Matter

Enhances Aesthetics of Garden

There are three times a year we should concern ourselves with mulching or re-mulching our gardens; early **Spring**, the dead of **Summer** and a couple of weeks **before** the first freeze.

Let's talk about mulching in a normal calendar year and assume all of our nasty winter weather has run its course. Usually, *by the end of February, or the first of March*, if you're not thinking of the work that must be done in and around the landscape, your spouse probably is. So, when you go out to buy new plant material, this is the time to stock up on the mulch as well.

Do me a favor, and pick up **four bags more** than you think you need. Few if any average gardeners ever pick up enough bags of mulch and tend to spread what they have too **thin.** And, a serious rain storm comes through and washes it away.

Our second time of the year that mulching should be done, is *during the heat of summer.* By now, temperatures are 90° or above and drought stress is a real possibility. If you have those extra bags from early spring, use them. If you're going out to buy some summer annuals or new plant material, get four to six new bags of mulch. Hopefully, you'll have enough left over for fill-in purposes once rains ramble through.

Finally, *before* winter sets in, mulch every part of the garden maintaining a thick layer of mulch. This will keep all the plant roots insulated from serious freezes and continue to help retain valuable moisture, especially when we tend to forget to *irrigate* during the months of December and January.

> *Two inches* is always a safe bet for mulch thickness. Don't exceed it, but never short-change yourself with only a ½" either.

NOW, what *kind* of mulch is best for your garden or landscape? There are more types of mulching material available to the average gardener than ever before. Most are helpful in the conservation, insulation and weed prevention factors we desire, while others are *better* suited for specific applications.

MULCHING MATERIAL

There are twelve mulching materials we can use in our gardens, but there are really only **five** that would fit into the GGG philosophies of **ease-of-use** and **low cost**. Those would be:

Pine Bark Mulch—is one of the most attractive of all the mulches and stays in place better than most. However, it is slow to break down into the ultimately beneficial humus we desire in our gardens. Pine Bark **Nuggets** last the longest, but they don't break down at all and they tend to wash away the easiest in heavy rains. Pine Bark Mulch is best used around trees and shrubs.

Shredded Hard Wood Mulch—There two very distinct hard wood mulches. One is shredded fine enough that it is ready for composting. The other has more solid wood pieces and will take much longer to break down into humus. They are both quite attractive. And there is a company in Houston, **Living Earth Technologies**, that by far, makes the best looking Shredded Hard Wood Mulch I have ever used. They take great pride in their ability to provide extremely useable mulches for the average homeowner.

Another reason you want somewhat *composted*

Shredded Hard Wood Mulch is that fresh chips from recently processed trees can introduce unwanted pests and diseases.

Shredded Hard Wood Mulch is best used around trees, shrubs, perennial and annual beds.

Leaves/Grass Clippings—These should be composted almost immediately. However, if time is a problem, these provide excellent mulching sources for instant use. Leaves are a great insulator around flower beds and vegetables gardens—but they do blow away easily. It's a smart move to mix them with dried grass clippings. Now, do you want to go to all the trouble of drying grass clippings before making them a mulch? I didn't think so. That's why it's the GGG advice to compost them. They also work well as a fine mulch and insulator for flower beds and vegetable gardens.

Pine Needles—These too are slow to decompose but they are also long-lasting in that the tangled mesh they make helps keep them from blowing or washing away in stormy conditions. They're also good at suppressing weeds. Case in point: Think about areas in the forest where there are lots of pine trees. Where there are lots of needles on the ground, there are few weeds. Some people are paranoid about using pine needles because of their acid content. Well, the *dose* is the difference.

More than a couple of inches of pine needles could mean *too much acid* activity in the soil. However, pine needles are the *perfect* mulch for *acid-loving* plants like Azaleas, Camellias and Roses.

Composted Humus—The irony of composted humus material is it takes *extra effort* to develop your own compost pile, which translates into more work and less time on the golf course. Still, well-composted humus is the best mulch around, but it breaks down almost too quickly for the GGG faithful. So, while I encourage the use of compost piles, I will understand if you have to buy your own bags of humus material to get in that full 18. (A round of golf, for those who couldn't guess.)

Other mulches that **do not** fit the GGG mold, but are available nonetheless:

Straw/Hay
Newspaper
Crushed Rock
Clear Plastic
Black Plastic
Landscape Fabric
Kiln Fired Rocks (Permanent Amendment Like Soil Pro 600)

MULCH RINGS AROUND TREES

Twenty years ago, the kind of mulches we've been talking about weren't used extensively in Texas gardens. Today, most people are seeing it used as an afterthought to most landscaping jobs. But eventually it will be the driving thought of many landscape jobs, mainly because of its great list of benefits. Another venue I see is a big market for pine bark, shredded hard wood, and pine needle mulches in the future as decorative paths and barren covers.

Another commonly asked question on my radio show is, "How can I get grass to grow under my shade tree where there are lots of tree roots." Well, *never*, is pretty much a safe answer, but what I've been trying to explain to people is the benefit of not trying to get grass to grow there anyhow, rather look at what we can do with mulches as far as rings around the tree base, walking paths, and generally decorative purposes.

Can you envision looking under a 40-year-old Live Oak at a winding path or dark, rich-looking mulch that winds gracefully around this massive oak. On various sides are concrete and wooden potters filled with shade-loving tropical plants and beautiful annuals of contrasting reds, pinks and whites. Then as your eyes move along, on the other side of the winding mulch path sits a wooden park bench with beige flower pots adorned with lion's faces and filled with bright yellow and orange annuals

The point is, be different. Create! Innovate! Enjoy experimenting! You don't have to plant grass, nor do you have to have some sort of flower bed under the tree.

Golf Tip #3:

The longer you wait for a player out in front to clear for your shot, the more errant your shot will become.

Part 4

Shrubs

Since Texas has a wide range of climates and soil conditions, the suggestions for plant material are chosen to excel in two specific regions; from a range just west of San Antonio to the Texas/Louisiana border. Then, north and south from about Bryan/College Station to the Corpus Christi area.

The key to making these plant suggestions work, is to follow the correct *sunlight exposure*. They will be grouped into plants that love FULL SUN, plants that thrive in PARTIAL SHADE (which, loosely defined, means full morning sun and partial protection from the hot midday sun).

And finally, those plants that need SHADE, or very little direct sunlight. Nevertheless, they can take bits of filtered sunlight through trees and structures.

It's also important to remember that shrubs, not trees, are the main element of any landscape. And not only will well-placed and cared for shrubs provide aesthetic beauty, they can also help screen, shade and protect your home. Another important factor to remember when selecting shrubs is that they come in all sizes, shapes, colors and textures. So, picking three different plants that end up growing at the same height and are all dark green in foliage defeats the purpose of having so many to choose from.

Although this book tells you how to spend the **minimum** amount of time in the garden from month to month, remember many of the best landscape plants are very water-efficient. It really isn't until *after* their establishment period do they require minimal water from the hose or irrigation system. So, no matter what you transplant, consistent

watering for the first 2-3 months of the plant's transplant-life is critical.

Your long-term success and ultimate satisfaction with these plants will also be based largely on how much attention you give to the condition of the planting situation as well. That's why it's imperative that you commit Part 5 on soil preparations to memory along with mulching in Part 3.

FULL-SUN PLANTS

Abelia
Boxleaf Euonymus
Burford Holly
California Fan Palm✶
Coppertone Loquat (Shrub)✶
Crimson Pigmy Barberry
Dwarf Chinese Holly
Dwarf Pittosporum
Dwarf Yaupon Holly
Elaeagnus
Gardenia
Hibiscus✶

Indian Hawthorn
Japanese Boxwood
Junipers
Lavender Tree (Vitex) Crape Myrtle
Loquat Tree✶
Lorapetulum (Witch Hazel or Fringe Flower)
Nandina
Oleander
Pampas Grass
Photinia
Pindo Palm✶
Pittosporum
Privet
Rose of Sharon (Althea)

Sago Palm
Spiraea
Texas Mountain Laurel
Texas Sage
Texas Sabal Palm✶
Tinus Viburnum
Waxleaf Ligustrum

✶ Subject to freeze damage

PARTIAL SHADE PLANTS

You'll notice some similar plants from the Sun-Loving List. That means they'll work well in either situation.

Asparagus Fern
Azalea
Boxleaf Euonymus
Camellias
Cleyera
Coral Honeysuckle
Cotoneaster
Dwarf Nandina
Dwarf Burning Bush
Gardenia
Giant Liriope
Hydrangea
Japanese Holly

Needlepoint Holly
Nellie R. Stevens Holly
Pigmy Date Palm✳
Pyracantha (Firethorn)
Sago Palm
Spiraea
Viburnum
Waxleaf Ligustrum
Windmill Palm
Yaupon Holly

✳ Subject to freeze damage

TOTAL SHADE PLANTS

You might notice one or two carry-overs from the Partial Shade group and one plant from the Total Sun group as well.

Ajuga
Algeria Ivy
Aspidistra (Cast Iron Plant)
Azaleas
Cleyera
Crotons✳
Dogwood
Dwarf Nandina
Giant Liriope
Gold Dust Aucuba
Holly Fern

Japanese Holly
Japanese Yew
Monkey Grass
Needle Point Holly
Oregon Grape Holly
Sago Palm
Taxus
Viburnum

✳ Subject to freeze damage

If you ask a sports enthusiast what their favorite team is, they will not hesitate to tell you. Furthermore, they probably won't give it a second thought to tell you all the *pros* and *cons* of why they do and/or don't like a particular team. Since I'm not a sportswriter, but rather a gardening writer, please indulge me this time to explain to you my list of favorite landscape shrubs.

In alphabetical order refer to the earlier lists to confirm sunlight requirements if it doesn't become clear in the descriptions of each of these GGG favorites.

B oxleaf Euonymus—This is a low growing shrub with dark green leafs that at first glance look somewhat like a darker, richer version of the Japanese Boxwood. It should only be used as a low-growing hedge or border, but can stand alone in an informal, loosely structured garden. It will get no bigger than two feet high and two feet wide. It is tolerant to our heat and poor soils, but it is susceptible to powdery mildew and scale insects.

C amellias—So many good things to mention, so little space. One caveat, since the Camellia needs an acid soil, iron supplementation and specific feedings, it doesn't necessarily fit perfect GGG criterion. However, even if you didn't do the acid, iron or fertilizer ever, while you may not get good flowers, you still have an evergreen plant that can grow as tall as five feet and do well in the shadier and controlled sunlight areas. The best thing about camellias; beautiful, rose-like flowers from November through February, when we have little other landscape color. **Excellent** accent plant, but *never* a good plant for hedges or borders.

C **leyera**—The best all around plant no matter the light condition. They do, however, *excel* in areas of limited sunshine but also my top recommendation when people want to plant an evergreen in a shady environment. The glossy green foliage often gives way to bronze-red tips when the plant is young, and needs little if any pruning from year to year. It will grow slower than, but is much like a *Red Tip Photinia* or a *Ligustrum* so can be used as a hedge or can even stand alone.

C **oppertone Loquat**—A hedge version of the popular Loquat trees that provides coppery and bronze looking leaf tips on new growth, much like *Red Tip Photinias*. Since it is a fairly new introduction to SE Texas nurseries, it is not found everywhere. Although it is used as a screen and hedge like a Waxleaf Ligustrum, it doesn't have as dense a growth, simply because it's leaves are big and awkward from its Loquat ancestry. They will probably never get any taller than 5 feet, but can be maintained for their first few years in the 2-3 foot range.

    The biggest **drawback** to Coppertone Loquats is they are susceptible to serious freeze damage when temperatures drop below 25°. In those cases, just cover them with blankets and they'll usually survive.

C **rape Myrtle**—You can now find crape myrtles in weeping forms and dwarf forms. Whatever size you decide, there is nothing more beautiful in the harsh summer landscapes of SE Texas than a wide variety of colors bursting from Crapes. They need total sun, and can take any amount of punishment you can deal out from lack of water, to excessive pruning. While they are susceptible to powdery mildew and insect pressures, they will mostly survive all of these threats without ever needing treatment. However, they also respond quickly and positively to proper treatments.

D warf Pittosporum (Wheeler's Pittosporum)—The only "Pitt" I can ever advise getting. Regular pittosporums were over-used in Texas landscapes since the 1950s. However, the Dwarf (or Wheeler's) Pitt stays extremely compact and mounded. They can be trimmed occasionally for control purposes and they provide an almost *yellowish* leaf contrast to the many other dark green evergreens gardeners want. Dwarf Pitts are a popular selection for low-growing borders, but they are becoming even more popular as a unique groundcover.

E laeagnus—Prized for its fast growth, while its maximum height will probably be six feet. And its biggest asset is a toss up between the fact that it thrives in poor soil, or that it has distinctive silvery-green foliage, which is striking against standard evergreens. Elaeagnus can also be used as a fast growing screen, and its tiny little flowers produce a nice fragrance.

H ibiscus—This is one of the showiest of all the flowering shrubs we can care for. Its biggest drawback is its easy freeze factor. It never takes much to knock back every leaf and every branch. But wait till next spring, well-mulched Hibiscus always tend to come back. They thrive in Texas heat and there are so *many* colors to choose from. They also make perfect accent shrubs, and they excel as large potted plants. If you lose them to freezes every year, just consider them big old annuals.

J **apanese Yew**—Need a plant that can be shaped to your specifications and fill in a very narrow, albeit tall niche in the garden??? Get a Japanese Yew! It can grow in any light condition from shade to full sun. Yews make a good contrast to standard evergreen shrubs in tiered situation because they can grow as high as 10 to 12 feet. Its acceptance to pruning helps it fit those specific areas. Some yews are even grown out to be large topiaries.

L **orapetulum** (Chinese Fringe Flower)—Actually, the Lorapetulum was always known as *Witch Hazel*, but years of varietal breeding has given us what marketers are now calling the *Chinese Fringe Flower*. They come in different flowering colors from purple to red to white. They will be more readily available from 1997 on as a non-standardized bedding plant, mainly because of their graceful arching branches and continual blooms.

N **andina** (Heavenly Bamboo)—Gets its nickname from the almost bamboo-looking, cane-like stems that form once the plant has been established. The strong selling points for Nandinas are that they can be trimmed for shape constantly, and their unique colors. The delicate foliage will turn brilliant shades of red, purple, orange and yellow from fall through the winter, even when stressed. That obviously makes the Nandina another good contrast plant for tiered situations against standard evergreens. They can grow as tall as six feet, but can also be controlled to stay in the 2-3 foot range.

Needlepoint Holly—Most nurseries stock Burford Hollies. I suggest you settle for nothing less than the *Needlepoint Holly!* They grow faster than the Burfords and their pointed leaves are always more supple than Burfords and old-style multi-point hollies. Needlepoints work best in shadier areas, which quite possibly get a couple of hours of morning sun. They can grow up to eight feet if left alone, but they can also be shaped much like a Ligustrum or Photinia hedge, but *do* have a much darker leaf.

Photinia (Red Tip Photinias)—Another in a long line of fast-growing shrubs that are probably best used as hedges and borders. Photinias are prized for their spectacular red leaf tips new to the growth in spring and fall. They are extremely heat tolerant and need mostly sun to thrive. But they need good drainage and are extremely susceptible to fungal leaf spots. Avoid this future problem by requesting new hybrid varieties that are resistant to the dreaded fungal leaf spot.

Privets (Vicary Privet)—What makes the privet work so well in our SE Texas landscapes is that it grows so fast, but will stop at four to five feet. Privet's also have a beautiful golden to olive green foliage. They provide an instant and striking contrast to most standard evergreens. And they do well in sunny conditions and poor soils. For a screen for something like a utility box or a low window, **Vicary Privet!**

Sago Palm—Probably one of the most sought after landscape pieces since the late 1980s. It is a very slow-growing palm-like plant that looks exceptional as accents in any landscape, and also do well in patio pots. This is an all-star selection, in that it too can do well in just about any light condition from shade to full sun. I recommend full sun as much as possible. The neatest thing about established Sagos, is how they develop multiple trunks by sending "pups" out year after year. They are usually as tall as they are wide, and most often peak at 5-6 feet both ways.

Snow Hawthorn—This is a white-flowered Indian Hawthorn. While I would prefer the pink flowers over the white ones on any day, it's the consistent rounded growth that I prefer with the white versions of Hawthorns. Pink ones always tend to get leggy, or, don't fill in well and do not fill in as well as the Snow's do. I love all Hawthorns for the distinctive leathery leaves they provide, and the fact that they can do well in full sun to partial sun. They should get no bigger than three feet tall and three feet wide. Perfect for mass planting needs.

Texas Sage—Another of the rounded shrubs that provide unique silvery leaves. Biggest benefit: The beautiful orchid-lavender bell-shaped flowers. They too can tolerate our poor soil conditions, and they too can provide a needed contracts in front of or behind standard evergreens. Can be used as a hedge, but I recommend it as a single piece in a mixed, informal landscape.

Waxleaf Ligustrum—An oldie, but a goodie! If planted properly is still one of the fastest growing shrubs around. The glossy light green leaves can be used to contrast extremely dark green shrubs. But the Ligustrum's strongest point are: (a) Dense compact growth that can reach as high as 10 feet. Probably the standard of all hedge plants back in the 1960s and 1970s. (b) Ligustrums can be trained into hour glass shapes, or globes and even specimen trees no taller than 8-10 feet.

OTHER GOOD SMALL SHRUBS/GROUNDCOVERS

Aztec Grass
Giant Liriope
Holly Ferns
Monkey grass
Mondo Grass
Variegated Liriope

UNDESIRABLE SMALL SHRUBS/GROUNDCOVERS

Plants that do **not** subscribe to GGG philosophies: In other words, I **don't, won't** and **never WILL** use them in my landscape.

arberry—Ugly! Not only when its growing its unique maroon-colored leaves, but extremely ugly in the winter when it loses all of its leaves. It always comes back, but tell me it doesn't look like a dead bush left to its own devices each winter? Pass it up.

ird of Paradise—A tropical plant that excels in South Texas, but not always here because of it's susceptibility to freeze damage. Prized for its unique flowers, they require inordinate amounts of water and do best when grown outside, which makes it an effort in futility for many SE Texas gardeners.

Golden Euonymus—They have a distinctly yellow/green color. BUT THEY NEVER GROW. And they are extremely susceptible to *euonymus scale.*

atal Plums—Extremely subject to freeze damage. It is only recommended by certified nursery professionals for the Rio Grand Valley. Can even die back when temperatures dip just below 40°.

Pampas Grass—GGG disciples will agree, that Pampas Grass has wreaked havoc on many golfers. Thus, as a golfer, I want nothing to do with it in my landscape, no matter now fast it grows and distinctive looking it is. But, for a golfer's **yard**, decide for yourself. It literally needs NO maintenance and can grow in concrete (well, almost).

Queen Palm—Another *freeze-susceptible* plant. If you're willing to wrap and unwrap the trunk each time the temperature gets to freezing then by all means, get one! **But**, if you forget to wrap it, you are subject to freeze damage of the trunk and the tree will most likely die. If you forget to unwrap it when things warm up, you suffocate the trunk. Big headache for golfers.

Golf Tip #4:

Train your pet goldfish to retrieve balls if you don't want to get wet.

Part 5

Soils

PLANTING IN TEXAS GUMBO
(Not a cookbook chapter)

Soil is produced when parent materials are acted upon by climate and vegetation over a period of time. It consists of weathered rock fragments with decaying organic matter. Soil also contains varying proportions of air water and micro-organisms. *Yawnnn!!!* That's not what you want to know about soil, is it? I didn't think so. What you do need to know is that the right kind of soil, for whatever outdoor bed you desire, will eliminate many future headaches. We will also examine the proper soil for indoor plants, but for now, let's really concentrate on outdoor beds.

RAISED BEDS

If you want to save valuable time in your future gardening endeavors, take this critical time now to prepare the right soil conditions. In this part of the state, most of our soils aren't too good. In fact, it's pitiful. That's because it's mostly clay. Some people have *gumbo,* some have *caleche,* some sandy-loam with a preponderance of clay. Whatever the case, it's seldom the optimum planting material. And that's why we have to improve almost any soil situation before we plant a seed, a flower, a shrub or a tree.

In almost any case, we need to create raised beds on top of our existing soil. However, it's also extremely important to work the two together, eventually making a new flower bed, shrub bed or vegetable garden raised a minimum of 6-8", while 8-10" raised beds will work even better. This almost always means adding a myriad of top soils, sands, organic matter and amendments.

If you do not have what is referred to as a *loamy soil*, and few people in these parts do have such soil, the key for successful GGG followers is to make sure the soil we add is mixed equally with top soil, sand and humus material. To make the proper raised bed, throw down a 2-3" layer of this soil/sand/humus mix, which we'll refer to from now on as a **Garden Mix**, and till it into the existing, compacted soil, then apply the rest and till the entire raised bed again. Now, you have successfully created a raised bed.

The average root system of any five gallon or smaller shrub will work beautifully in this mix. There is a need for light compacting of the area before the entire planting process, but the bottom line is now you have a *rich planting environment* that will continue to improve with the addition of humus material over the years. As time passes, the break-down of organic matter and constant microbial activity of the humus material will continue to improve your soil inches below that original excuse for soil that we know as clay.

For years, I have read and written technical books and papers about soils and their properties, and while we could spend time discussing basic soil composition, its pH level, its nutrient needs and nutrient makeup, what you would learn is that to be a successful gardener (yet create more time for golf) remember the basics of a **raised bed**. It should start with a Garden Mix of soil; raise the beds a minimum of 6" all the way up to 12"; and continue to add mulch so that it can continually add to the organic and beneficial makeup of your soils. But for the purposes of succeeding with raised beds, remember that adding mulch three times a year will be a key to continued and successful development of proper soils.

If you are in a quandary as to how much Garden Mix you will need to raise your beds, here is a basic rule. First remember that soil is mostly sold by the *cubic yard* and in order to **raise** your soil level by 4", you will need to **divide** the square footage of the area you're working by 73. That number will help determine the cubic yards needed. Then remember that you will need **two times** that amount for an 8" raised bed, and **three** times that amount for a 12" raised bed.

> For Example: My square footage for gardening in raised beds is 150 square feet (5 feet wide and 30 feet long). Divide 150 by 73 and you've got about 3.2 cubic yards. For an **8**" raised bed we need 7 cubic yards and over 10 cubic yards for a 12" raised bed in the 150 square feet of space allotted.

Now that's a lot of soil, because 150 square feet is a big bed. But if you're dealing with anything over 2 cubic yards of soil anyway, you will need to go to a soil yard or have it delivered, because buying pre-mixed soil (with the requirements given above) can get expensive. It's always cheaper to buy it in bulk.

Now that I've hopefully convinced you of a Garden Mix and the benefits of raised bed, let's also go through some additional, and common sense steps when building these beds. While some may seem obvious, they're still worth mentioning.

✔Remove all grass, rocks/debris before you till up the soil

✔Never till up wet soil

✔In most cases, there will still be a need to fertilize plants and flowers, normally with **slow release** *1-2-1* ratios or balanced *1-1-1* ratios. They could be *12-24-12* or *13-13-13* for example.

✔Additional soil activators or micro-nutrients added from year to year help in maintaining active soils. *Medina Soil Activator* and *Super Thrive* are good examples of some brand name soil enhancers. This DOES NOT include root stimulators.

✔Pay attention to the pH needs of the plants you choose. Remember, acid-loving plants need **additional** acid and iron, that do not come naturally or even in the raised beds you've made. *Azaleas, Camellias* and *Gardenias* are good examples.

✔If you live in the *Piney Woods*, or along the *Gulf Coast* and think your soil is more sandy than clay, you will need **less** sand in the Garden Mix for raised beds. Such mixes can be made specifically to your desire at soil yards.

PLANTING MEDIUM FOR INDOOR PLANTS

Much like the soil for our outdoor beds, the proper mix of potting soil, sand and humus material is paramount to successful indoor plants. The difference here is that there is less of a need for top soil and humus material.

The first key to a potting medium for indoor plants,

however, is drainage. **Too much drainage** means frequent waterings and insufficient room for root systems to take hold. **Too little drainage**, often means that the much needed moisture isn't getting to the root mass. Refer to Part 8 for more in-depth discussion of indoor plants.

If you're going to be successful with indoor plants, one of the first things you must often do is replant the specimen into the proper soil. The soft, fluffy material come in is inadequate at best. The reason it is so porous when your buy it is because the nurseries or greenhouses can water on a daily basis. I know of few people who want to continue watering their plants on a daily basis once they get them home.

The best shortcut I can suggest is to an **organically-based potting medium**. The company, *Humusoil,* has created an organic potting medium that I consider perfect for indoor tropicals and hanging baskets. I've seen it at many nurseries labeled simply as *Organic Potting Soil*. It's the optimum mix of soil, sand and finely composted humus material. It holds plenty of water for the entire root system, with the sand creating a perfect flow throughout the entire medium.

If you want to create your own, it is critical to visualize 1/3 of your potting medium as a combination of sharp sand and organic material like well-composted humus. In lieu of well-composted humus, you can also incorporate a generous portion of a permanent soil amendment like **Soil Pro 200**™ *or* **Super Dirt**™. If you can find *perlite* or *vermiculite* instead of the permanent soil amendments just mentioned, they will work too.

But the quickest shortcut to successful soils for **indoor plants** is the **organically based potting soils already pre-**

mixed and in bags! I often tear little holes in bags to look at the makeup of the potting medium. What you are looking for is that balance between soil, sand and humus material. If it looks too fluffy, like the medium the plant comes in, move on.

Hopefully, you have also seen tips on television or in books that show the importance of drainage at the bottom of each pot you are planting in. For years, horticultural experts have encouraged the use of shards of clay pots at the bottom of these pots. This is still the most tried and true method. But I've discovered and have had a great deal of success with broken pieces of brick, small rocks and big chunks of decorative bark mulch.

If you use the bark mulch pieces, be prepared to replant every couple of years. That's because they will break down eventually losing their ability to create the drainage zone at the bottom of the pot.

It is equally as important to make sure that there is usually **more than one drainage hole** at the bottom of plastic or clay pots. In many cases, there is only one tiny hole and with some plastic planters, there are often 2 or 3 tiny holes that should be expanded.

Golf Tip#5:

Despite what your significant other says; Golf is not a four letter word.

Part 6

Native Texas Plants

THE NATURAL GARDEN

If it grows in the wild, why can't I just plant one in my yard and leave it alone? That sounds like a fair question, doesn't it? I mean if it grows natively, or is indigenous to our part of the world, why in the world does it need watering, or for that matter fertilizing? What you don't realize is how many seedlings **didn't** make it, and how many trees died off from drought, insect or fungal pressures. Still, it's a fair assessment and an idea whose time has come.

We all need to know which native Texas plant species work best in this area. Texas has up to 8 very distinct regions in which there are countless native species per region. As a whole, there are more than 5,000 native Texas species. But, armed with the knowledge found here, you can start looking for native species to plant in the garden, that with a little boost in their early lives, can and thrive with little if any care later in life.

I'm not asking you to commit your entire landscape to natives, but start incorporating them little by little until you've got what might be considered a "natural" garden. As the years move on, I'm finding more and more landscapers moving away from formal gardens based in the old English style of beds and borders, and opting for a relaxed alternative and that's where natives are so helpful. That is also where the knowledge of natives comes in handy.

Plus, it will be beneficial to have a natural garden take its design suggestions from *Mother Nature*. To create a naturalistic garden of Texas natives it helps to study an area where nature remains undisturbed. Search for these natural areas that are similar to your existing soil and moisture types, because it doesn't make a whole bunch of sense to rate plants in a wet area if your property is dry. Right?

Yes, the eventual establishment of predominant native Texas plants helps you cut back on long-term care needs which means not only a cutback on water, its pest and disease resistance but also adapting to the vagaries of your soil and irrigation needs. This chapter isn't a lecture about committing yourself to natives, just some alternatives that can be helpful to GGG followers by slowly adapting a garden to lower maintenance plants. You are about to see four distinct lists of natives indigenous to four regions that overlap Central to Southeast Texas. Use them as guide-posts when looking for new plant material.

Southeast Texas actually has four of the eight growing regions. There's the **Coastal Plains**, the **Piney Woods,** the **Post Oak Plain** and the **Blackland Prairies,** just Northwest of the Houston area.

The following list is a compilation of trees, shrubs, vines and perennials that do well in all four of these locations, with a greater emphasis of native species that thrive in the Houston soils and climate.

And remember this is an informal list compiled alphabetically per region.

Houston Coastal Plains

American Beautyberry
Bald Cypress
Black Gum
Blue Texas Star
Carolina Jessamine
Coralberry
Crinum Lily
Flameleaf Sumac
Fringe Tree
Inland Seaoats
Lady Fern
Mexican Plum
Palmetto
Parsley Hawthorn
Possumhaw

River Birch
Rusty Blackhaw Viburnum
Sensitive Fern
Southern Magnolia
Swamp Chestnut Oak
Texas Hibiscus
Titi
Turk's Cap
Virginia Sweetspire
Wax Myrtle
Western Mayhaw
White Oak
Wild Ageratum
Wood Fern
Yaupon Holly

Piney Woods

Beech
Blue Jasmine
Blue Texas Star
Carolina Rose
Dwarf Wax Myrtle
Flameleaf Sumac
Partridgeberry
Sassafrass
Spiderwort
Widow's Tears

Blackland Prairie

American Holly
Arkansas Yucca
Azalea
Bracken
Carolina Buckthorn
Chain Fern
Chalk Maple
Coral Honeysuckle
Eastern Red Cedar
Falkenberry
Fringe Tree
Mapleleaf Viburnum
Mayapple
Oklahoma Plum
Palmetto
Pine Trees
Pinewoods Lily

Red Maple
Shumard Red Oak
Snowbell
Southern Arrowood
Southern Sugar Maple
Southern Magnolia
Swamp Chestnut Oak
Trillum
Texas Wisteria
Turk's Cap
Two Winged Silverbell
Violets
White Oak
Wood Fern
Yaupon Holly
Zig Zag Iris

Post Oak Plains

You'll notice not as many specimens, but more wildflower production.

American Beautyberry
Arkansas Yucca
Black-Eyed Susan
Bitterweed
Bluebonnet
Butterfly weed
Coralberry
Diamond Petal Primrose
Eastern Red Cedar
Ebony Spleenwort
Eryngo

Flowering Dogwood
Fragrant Phlox
Horsemint
Indian Blanket
Indian Paintbrush
Lazy Daisy
Mexican Plum
Partridge Pea
Possumhaw
Post Oak
Prairie Flameleaf Sumac (Meadow of Wildflowers)
Redbud
Ruellia
Rusty Blackhaw Viburnum
Snow-on-the-Mountain
Smooth Sumac
Spiderwort
Violet
Virginia Creeper
White Oak
Widow's Tears
Yaupon Holly

Please don't hesitate to invest in a spectacular book known as *Native Texas Plants; Landscaping Region by Region* by *Sally* and *Andy Wasowski*. In my estimation, it is the definitive written resource on Texas native plants. Not only is it well written, it is beautiful just to browse through. There are innovative uses for hundreds of the native landscape plants they describe. And they've broken it down to 8 different planting regions, one of which, is your own.

Part 7

Lawns

TURFGRASS

Before I started working in Houston to dispense gardening advice as a radio broadcaster, I got a lot of questions from my neighbors in Bryan (Texas) about what I did to make my lawn greener and keep it greener longer than theirs? Also, what did I do to keep weeds from infiltrating my lawn? What I told them is what I'm telling you, there is not one universal answer.

The most interesting thing I've learned since I started writing about horticulture and agriculture is there are many solutions to most problems. It was interesting how differently homeowners fertilize their yards and farmers their agronomic crops; everyone knew **the best** way to do it. I guess "the best way" is whatever works for you and it just shows how much information is out there concerning the practice of fertilization.

One of my mentors at Texas A&M University, *Dr. Richard Duble,* is the **preeminent turfgrass authority** in the state of Texas. That's saying a lot, because there are so many different growing regions in the state. There's fescues in El Paso, to Buffalo Grasses in the Rio Grande Valley, to Zoysias in Dallas. And this information on turfgrasses is ever-evolving, thanks to researchers like Dr. Duble, which means this information today might not be valid 20 years from now.

But I am sure you're not as interested in as much

textbook jargon as you are in straight talk. And that's what I will try to supply in this GGG chapter on your lawn.

Since turfgrasses are often the greatest percentage of front and back lawns, I'm going to shower you with tips, some shortcuts, and the most current scientific information that will help you attain a green, lush, weed-free lawn!

FERTILIZER

The **most important** thing to do when purchasing fertilizer, is to **NOT** look for the cheapest. Just because one of those big mega-stores has a tremendous price on fertilizer does not mean it's best for your yard. It is **far wiser** to pay a couple more bucks per bag to get a **premium product** that has been devised for this region! If the product was produced in the South, then it was probably researched for application on southern lawns.

The **cheapest** bags of fertilizer usually come from somewhere outside of the state of Texas. Look at the fine print on the back. Those produced in Gulf Coast states are probably good enough. But what if it was produced in Pennsylvania or Ohio? Chances are slim that they truly understand our growing conditions both agronomically and climatically. It won't be **bad** for your lawn, just not as good.

RATIOS/N-P-K

What kind of fertilizer and what ratio should I use? 3-1-2 is the answer but refer to the next chapter, please! Boy, if it was truly that easy! This is the **next best** piece of information you need to be armed with when you go to your lawn and garden store for fertilizer. Funny thing is, you'll probably never see a bag that has the exact numbers 3-1-2. You'll see **21-7-14, 15-5-10, 19-5-9, 19-6-10** as examples. Those are good examples of 3-1-2 ratios. If you'll notice, the last two examples aren't mathematically correct, they are nearly *4-1-2* ratios. However, those too are good for Southern lawns; we can benefit from more nitrogen than phosphorous and potassium.

Oops! Sometimes I assume that everyone knows what I'm talking about with regard to the *Nitrogen-Phosphorous-Potassium* configuration or the **N-P-K.** Which is what the 3-1-2 is based on. *Nitrogen* is first, *Phosphorous* is second and *Potassium* third.

Nitrogen provides for the green surge in the grass when used properly and evenly. Biologically, nitrogen is a part of chlorophyll and has a great deal to do with the growth of every plant, but even more importantly for grasses.

Phosphorous is essential for good root growth. However, research has shown that phosphorous moves slowly over the years and even slower in **clay** soils. Instead of a 13-13-13 (or a 1-1-1 ratio), which was prescribed for years in Houston, we now know we have too much phosphorous because it just hasn't *moved*. Thus the advent of the 3-1-2 ratio.

Potassium has many roles. Its most important is with *water relations* within the plant. The proper amount of potassium helps protect the water needs during drought stresses and even in times of too much water.

The next best thing about premium lawn foods for Southern lawns, is that they also contain **trace minerals**, or **secondary plant food elements** which benefit our yards.

Elements like *Calcium, Sulfur, Magnesium, Iron, Copper, Manganese* and Zinc.

High-nitrogen fertilizers are bad for our Southern lawns. Well, it's not that they are bad, it's just, as a rule, we don't take proper **care** of turfgrasses after applying high-nitrogen doses. If we misapply water, or don't apply any at all, the grass gets burned. If we apply it at the wrong time, it does nothing and we wonder why it hasn't worked. Examples of *wrong* timing would be when the soil temperature hasn't reached 78° or above, or before a big rainstorm. High nitrogen mixes are seldom slow-release fertilizers, thus **cold** soil temperatures will never activate the nitrogen for the grass before it dissipates. Meanwhile, a gully-washer or a rainstorm simply washes the fast-release action right down the sewer.

Stay away from **high nitrogen fertilizers**, which would be *27-3-4, 30-5-5, or 24-1-3* as examples. The overall best piece of advice, stay away from **any** fertilizer that has its first number, or it's nitrogen allotment, higher than 21.

WHEN TO FERTILIZE

When to fertilize is just as important as **what** to fertilize with. My recommendation to apply that 3-1-2 slow release fertilizer **3 times** per year; one time in **April,** one time in **July,** and one time in **October** (preferably, the first week of those months). You may read in other garden books produced elsewhere that fertilizing four times a year is necessary. GGG disciples, listen to me. Three times a year is more than adequate.

You have probably seen (and will continue to see) neighbors applying fertilizer in March. I mean, after the freezes have passed and it proves to be a beautiful spring day, why not begin your yard work with a little fertilizing? **DON'T let the peer pressure get to you!** Go out and enjoy a round of golf instead. You must hold off until the **first week** in April.

Why? Because that's when I can all but guarantee that the soil temperature is finally going to be just right. If the soil temperature is too cold, you don't get the proper release of the many forms of slow-release nitrogen in a premium fertilizer. And it takes two good weeks of moderate temperatures (Highs in the 70s/80s and lows no lower than 60°) to warm the soil for perfect release.

So, repeat after me: I, (state your name) will enjoy the better things in life, like golf (or enter your favorite leisure activity here) as much as I can during the month of March and will not be tempted into fertilizing my lawn until the first of April.

If a good slow-release fertilizer feeds for 3-4 months, then the July fertilization is basically a mild overlap to the April application of premium lawn food. The July fertilization is also done with the premium 3-1-2. But now is when **irrigation** becomes more critical, because July, August and September are not the rainiest months around Texas.

The October fertilization is what we like to refer to as a *winterizer.* Most of the premium lawn food companies that produce the best 3-1-2 ratio fertilizers also produce a winter formulation that we put down in October. By and large, it is also fair game to put down a winterizer until we get our first frost. Some winterizers are *3-1-2* based some are *1-1-2* based. But the most important number to remember in winterizers is the last number-P, **Potassium!**

We still need our modicum of phosphorous for root

growth, but it's the potassium's work with water, or even lack thereof, that aids root growth during the winter. And remember, the healthier the root system coming out of winter, the quicker your grass will green back up in March. The nitrogen, in the best winterizers doesn't really promote rich, green growth. So, don't ever expect a surge of lush grass from October on. Instead, you are just looking to sustain a healthy root system.

This Texas weather is unpredictable. Best to turn to 740 on your AM radio dial Saturday thru Thursday from 10 'til noon for GardenLine and ask us about the weather and **exactly** when to do what; we'll tell you.

MOWING & MULCHING MOWERS

As disappointing as this may be, if you fertilize properly, you're going to need to **mow** the yard every now and then. It's entertaining to see how homeowners often take great pride in their front yards, so much so that mowing is sort of a territorial claim to their property. Everyone sees you working on your yard, and they see how neat and manicured it looks, reflecting positively on you and your family. (Do you **really** believe that?) If you can afford it, have someone else mow your grass and go play golf.

Now, if you're like me, and enjoy mowing the lawn for whatever reason, (I like the workout) the most important thing I can tell you these days is to use a **mulching mower** and please, **please, PLEASE** stop bagging your grass clippings. You can bag your grass clippings if, and only if, you have a compost pile. Despite the recent concerns of thatch build-up (which I will discuss a little later), mulch mowing is extremely beneficial for your grass and for our environment in general.

Why people still bag grass clippings and put them on the curb for the trash companies is beyond me. We already have over-stressed landfills, and oddly enough, some 30% of the trash going to these landfills in the spring and summer is **yard waste!** And while grass can breakdown in a landfill quite easily, the plastic bags do not. *Mulch-mowed* grass is beneficial for the yards because it is an instant and useable source of quick-release nitrogen!

THATCH

Thatch build-up has risen to mythical proportion in recent years. If your mulching mower is pulverizing the grass small enough you shouldn't have a problem with thatch for 20 years. Even then, a once-a-year, **aeration** also helps to prevent thatch build-up. Thatch occurs when our organic material from the mulching process is produced faster than it can decompose. A certain amount of thatch is desirable, because it works as a cushion for high-traffic areas and an insulator from extreme temperatures and reduces water evaporation.

The key is finding out if you have too much thatch. To do so, dig out a small square with dirt, roots and all. Look at the layer of organic material between the grass blades and the soil line. If it's thicker than ½" of organic matter, then aerate in the spring immediately following the scalping.

SCALPING

The what? The **scalping** is the usually the first mowing of the spring. You lower the mower an 1" to 1½" **below** your normal mowing height and **bag** all the dead grass and debris. Bags of scalped grass is the only other time we bag grass clippings outside those of us who maintain a compost pile. Not only does scalping remove the dead grass, but it opens the roots and soil to fresh air and sunshine. **WARNING:** If you scalp too soon and a freeze comes, the root system of the grass is extremely vulnerable. That's why we scalp **only** when we are **certain** that there are no more freezes. That's usually around March.

Immediately following the scalping, raise the mower back up. A rule of thumb is to set the mower high or almost as high as it will go. If your mower only has three settings, go as high as the settings will allow. But most mowers these days have 5-6 settings. The **higher** you set it the better off your grass will be and you don't have to mow as often.

It's also wise to have your lawnmower blades **sharpened** before first use each spring. It doesn't cost much and it helps maintain a consistency of mulched grass which helps reduce thatch.

WATERING

When we water the grass, it's important the water reaches to a depth of 4-6", to the root system. Repetitive, shallow waterings actually cause harm to the grass, mainly because the root systems starts looking for the moisture nearer the surface. Thus, the roots are vulnerable to heat and cold.

In lieu of a good rain storm once a week, we should be watering our grasses once a week with a **deep watering** that lasts 45 minutes to one hour. During the more stressful summer months like July and August, it's likely that such a watering practice will need to be moved up every 4-5 days, especially if there are no rains showers in sight. An application of 1" of irrigation water will work down 4-6" in a fertile yard. In most cases it takes some 45 minutes to achieve that inch. Here's how you can test for that inch of water.

Put out an empty coffee can or mason jar out three quarters of the way into the sprinkler's spray pattern. When it fills to one inch at the bottom you know how long it takes your system to apply the weekly one inch of water. Simple, huh?

Grass nearer to driveways and sidewalks will always **dry out** more quickly than the remainder of the lawn. These areas may need *supplemental irrigation* from time to time, to help keep the area moist and it will most assuredly help fight off chinch bugs.

LAWN

These are the **most insidious** bugs that terrorize the grass; *Chinch bugs, Grubs* and *Fire Ants.*

Chinch bugs often attack areas which have dried out, and are always a problem in Southeast Texas from about July through September. Their damage is fairly obvious as brown, discolored, irregular patches begin to form in the grass. And quite often that happens near sidewalks and/or driveways, or where there is a lack of water. If you can catch chinch bugs early enough, they can be treated with fertilizer! That's right, fertilizer! Because, in those browned out areas, there is also a lack of nitrogen. Treat with fertilizer and water heavily. Chinch Bugs **hate** water!

If the problem persists and the grass begins to die, you will need an **insecticide**. *Liquid Dursban* works best, because it breaks down in the environment. *Liquid Diazinon* also works, but if it's misapplied, it won't break down very well and then moves quite readily through the soils and into the drainage system causing problems for waste water treatment facilities. In either case, it usually takes at least two treatments 7-10 days apart for control. Please read and follow insecticide labels to the letter.

Grub worms or *White Grubs* are the larvae of *June Bugs* (June Beetles) . The larvae have black to gray heads with creamy white, fat, worm-like bodies. They are down-right repulsive looking. These grub worms feed on the root systems of grass. Their damage can often look like Chinch Bug damage, but if you don't find the chinch bugs as described earlier, look for grubs by peeling back a piece of sod. Look for these disgusting worms just below the root system. If you see more than four per square foot, treat with a granular *Dursban* so it can work through the root system to the soil below. Liquid insecticides are best for **topical** applications of insects on the grass blades.

To **control** Fire Ants, use a combination of liquid drenches and bait applications. Baits like *Amdro,* take a long time, but are effective long-term controls. Liquid drenches should be used on nuisance mounds that pop up somewhat overnight. Liquid drenches are *Dursban, Intercept*, or *Pyrethrins.*

DISEASES

I bet you can tell me the name of the BROWN, PATCHY-looking fungal disease that is the bane of most Houston gardeners. Did I give it away too easily? Yes, it's commonly referred to as **Brownpatch,** (*Rhizoctonia*) a fungal disease that appears in the form of yellowish, brown circles in the yards. It usually happens in the fall when cooler temperatures and moisture work together.

When I first began working for Texas A&M as a communications specialist in 1988, my father, a Houstonian since 1968, boldly told me that someone at A&M could make a fortune if they would figure out a way to control Brownpatch. He never really tried to control it with anything, because he knew his grass came back year after year. But little did he know that there were actually plenty of controls for the dreaded lawn "uglifier".

The key . . . is **timing!** If you use a **systemic fungicide** with *Bayleton* or *Benomyl* a month *before* the fungal spores get cracking, you can prevent it. If you want to **stop it in its tracks** because you are already **seeing** it, then a **contact fungicide** like *Daconil* or *Terraclor* works best.

There are other cultural practices we can incorporate to discourage Brownpatch. High nitrogen fertilizers **invite** the Brownpatch fungal disease. Improper drainage also encourages the disease, as does improper watering. What that means is water early in the morning, and allow the sun to dry the moisture before nightfall. Because it's the 60° nights and moist lawns in which Brownpatch flourishes.

Sadly, we are now being besieged with an even more insidious fungal disease known as **Take-All Patch**

(Gaeumannomyces grammis). This shows up much like Brownpatch, but if left untreated will actually kill a yard, whereas Brownpatch will not. It's also quite discouraging that there are few, if any, fungicides that can control Take-All Patch. In truth, since it is such a new disease, there is much to be learned. The best control method via fungicides is *Rubigan,* but it's expensive and hard to find. Most golf courses use it because they are licensed for its application and can afford the cost. Until something new comes along, the average homeowner is stuck controlling Take-All Patch with systemic lawn fungicides like *Benomyl* or *Bayleton.* Systemic means we have to **prevent** Take-All Patch with *Benomyl* or *Bayleton.* Once the fungal disease takes hold, it's almost impossible to control. What that means to many people affected by Take-All Patch is to dig up and start over.

Gray leaf spot *(Piricularia grisea)*Is another common fungal disease on southern lawns. Gray leaf spot causes oval or circular, tan-colored lesions with brown borders on the leaf of the blades of St. Augustine grass. In severe cases gray leaf spot, can kill a lawn. But to reduce the infestation, you simply need to avoid applying anymore fertilizer. But it can also be stopped in it's track with the fungicide *Daconil.*

Slime Mold—Is not a serious problem and will usually go away on its own. But since it looks so nasty you might not want it around for long. My buddy, Scooter, had this problem in his new house and it first freaked him out, because it really did look like someone had poured some oil in a big manhole-sized patch in his front yard, then kind of dusted it with salt and pepper. First remember it is not a life threatening problem for the turfgrass. While slime mold is a fungal disease in the soil, it actually shows that you have good microbial activity just below. If waiting a few weeks for it to go away naturally isn't in your cards, then you can spray a simple fungicide like *Consan Triple Action 20*. This will kill the fungal spores and you can wash away the slime mold the next day.

WEEDS

Any growing thing that you don't want!

Disease, insects and irrigation problems aside, the absolute worst problem we have in southern lawns would have to be weeds. They compete with the grass for sunshine, water and nutrients and they seem to propagate quicker than any grass we can produce.

The most effective weed control program requires that you know **which kind** of weed you're dealing with. There are *broad-leaf weeds, grassy weeds* and *sedges* (grasslike herbs usually found in watery places). The chemical controls for these three groups of weeds differ greatly.

It's important to note that *Grassy* weeds have jointed, hollow stems and leaf blade veins that are parallel to leaf margins; plus, they are usually longer than they are wide. In contrast, *Broadleaf weeds* often have showy flowers and shoot off a network of veins at diverse angles. Finally, *Sedges* have grass-like characteristics, but require different chemical controls. We normally put the hard-to-control Nutgrass into this category.

Broadleaf	Grassy	Sedges
Buttonweed	Annual Bluegrass	Purple Nutsedge
Burweed	Crabgrass	Yellow Nutsedge
Clover	Dallisgrass	
Dandelions	Goosegrass	
Henbit	Grassburs	
Spruge		

Most of the Broadleaf weeds in Texas can be controlled with any of the 2, 4-D post-emergent herbicides, which kill the offending weed and leave the grass completely alone. 2, 4-D herbicides are products like **Greenlight's** *Wipeout*, **Ortho's** *Weed-B-Gone,* and **Enforcer's** *Roots & All.*

Broadleaf weeds can also be prevented from germinating with a **pre-emergent herbicide**. But, they must be applied at the proper time. The best known pre-emergent controls for Broadleaf weeds are *Portrait* and *Gallery.* Applications should be done in October and then again in February/March.

Grassy weeds, once up, are nearly impossible to control. That's why it's imperative to control grassy weeds with pre-emergent herbicides **early** in the spring then once more in the summer for total control. The best known grassy weed, pre-emergent herbicides are *Balan, Betasan.* Post-emergence control is done with weed-killers like *Finale* or *Roundup*, but these post emergence sprays for grassy weeds also kill your grass.

Nutgrass is controlled with herbicides known as *Image* or another hard to find one called *Basagran. Image* is expensive but still the only truly effective control both as a post *and* pre-emergent herbicide for sedges like nutgrass.

Another weed that has developed quite a notorious reputation in Southern lawns in the past five years is **Virginia Buttonweed**. This too is hard to control once it has germinated, so early control is critical. And Buttonweed too is best controlled with *Image.*

LAWNS REFERENCE GUIDE

- Don't Buy Cheap Fertilizer; Buy Premium
- Make Sure the Fertilizer is Formulated for Southern Lawns
- Don't Buy Weed & Feed Combinations
- Use a *3-1-2* Slow Release Ratio Fertilizer
    (*21-7-14, 15-5-10, 19-5-9, 19-6-10*)
- Fertilize 3 times per year: April, July, October (Winterize in October)
- Try Pre-Emergent Herbicides to Prevent Weeds
- Control Existing Weeds with Post-Emergent Herbicides
- Use a Mulching Mower; Don't Bag Grass Clippings (Except when Scalping)
- Scalp the Grass to Remove Dead Grass Early in Spring
- Set Your Mower at its Highest Cutting Height
- Water the equivalent of 1" of Rain Per Week
- Water more often near concrete to fight off chinch bugs

If I've gotten you excited about the cultural practices of turfgrass, and you want to know more, you can get the in-depth version of what I've told you in Dr. Richard Duble's **Turfgrasses—Their Management and Use in the Southern Zone,** 2nd edition. This is *the* classroom text used at Texas A&M University for students in the Soil & Crop Sciences department. And it can be ordered through the Texas A&M University Press in College Station.

Part 8

House Plants

Mother Nature does not produce "house plants", *per se.* Most of the plants that we grow successfully indoors are actually native to an *outdoor* environment. But given the right atmospheric conditions, almost anything that **grows** can eventually be adapted to a "house plant."

To give you an idea of what I'm talking about, this revolution in plant acclimation gives us the ability to grow exotic bulbs in and out of season and we can often make some citrus trees provide us with year-round *lemon, lime,* and *satsuma oranges*.

Our houses are supposed to be our most comfortable environment, a haven where we retire after a hard days work. Our house usually has the most agreeable climate we experience day-in and day-out. That's because we can control the humidity and temperature. Interestingly enough, this is **not** the ideal environment for tropically-based indoor plants. If you want your plants to thrive indoors, you would need turn the living room into a greenhouse of sorts, and the plants would excel and you would be miserable.

Between these two extremes, we can create a climate where people and plants coexist and it doesn't take much effort to accomplish this. The trick is knowing that all houses have different atmospheres, and just because your neighbor is growing orchids and bulbs indoors, doesn't necessarily mean that you can in your house.

If you'd like to add *feeling* to your home, plants and a fireplace will do it. A bare room graced with a huge *ficus* or a cascading *fern* suddenly brings the house alive! Most people feel better, and are even *soothed* when they are surrounded by live indoor plants.

Following the GGG low-maintenance tenet, you should concentrate on those plants that sustain, and thrive, with *minimal* care. This doesn't mean buy a whole bunch of fake, plastic houseplants? *Pittooeeyy!* I have never found a synthetic plant that compares with a live one. A good collection of live plants also helps to cleanse the air in the home. Synthetic ones only gather dust.

To succeed with indoor house plants, follow these simple rules. To thrive, they need. . .

Drainage/Watering
Proper Potting Soil
Proper Light Requirements
Occasional Feedings

To grow these plants successfully, I'll provide you with a condensed list of those houseplants that thrive with very little care. And, if you consider yourself a *brown thumb*, you can get a good start with these easy-to-care-for house plants and work your way up from there.

Of the four key elements to successful indoor house plants, the first three (drainage, soil and light) are necessary and work together. You can have the proper **light** require-ment for the plant, but if your **drainage** is poor or you've planted in the **wrong medium**, the plant will not survive. Likewise, if your soil is correct but you've got a shade loving plant in direct sunlight, it too will eventually die.

DRAINAGE & WATERING

Improper watering and/or improper drainage is the **#1** reason the average house plant owner destroys their plants. It could be because of **over**-watering, or it could be from **under**-watering. But, unless you totally ignore your plants and they dry up and die, it's the over-watering that ends up being the most common malady. That's because the excess amount of water combines with improper drainage and forces the roots of the plant to rest in water, resulting in root rot.

So, how much water should you give your plants? It would be simple to say, once a week. But it's not *that* easy. Light factors, temperature, humidity, containers and indeed the type of plant in question all combine to alter the water requirements of each plant. Plus, flowering plants need more water than those with waxy leaves. Plants with large leaf surfaces need more water than succulents. And in the winter, **all** plants require less water, because of their semi-dormant state.

There's no need for you to become **overly educated** about water requirements because, despite all the gadgets that you can buy to help read soil moisture, it simply comes down to *using your eyes and your fingers.*

Assuming you're using the right soil in the first place, if your plant is drooping or wilting, chances are it needs water. But the **sight-method** alone doesn't always work. Thus, the most tried and true method of judging a plant's water needs is the **finger test**. You simply poke your index finger an inch or so down into the soil, and if it feels dry, add some water. If the soil is still wet, do not add water. And check the plant again every few days.

If you're like me, you'll water some plants once a week and some plants every three to four days because some *seem* dryer than others. But once established, it's a safe bet to perform the finger test on the plant's soil once a week as a good habit. It's also important to remember that when watering, give your plants a **thorough** soaking. If you only water the top couple of inches, the roots will never receive an adequate amount of water.

And that leads back to **proper drainage**. Assuming you have the proper planting mix, you must also create a drainage pattern at the bottom of whatever planter you use. Horticulturists on television, as well as authors of other books, sing the praises or broken pieces of *terra cotta* clay pots at the bottom to create good drainage. Excellent idea! In *lieu* of that, you can use broken pieces of brick, large pebbles, large chunks of decorative pine bark nuggets, broken twigs and pieces or woody branches. Any of these items placed at the bottom of every house plant container allows excess water to drain through.

Drainage proves two things: If it runs straight through, you've got the *wrong* potting medium. Change it! If it only trickles through, you've done well with your potting medium.

Finally, but not last in its importance, you need drainage **holes** at the bottom of each container. Normally, a single 1" hole is adequate. But, 3 or 4 ½" holes around the container's outer edges are best. You see, **small** holes far too often clog with decomposing humus material or bits of stems, etc. That's why it's nearly as critical to have at least

½" circumference holes at the bottom of the container as it is to have the buffer material like the broken pieces of terra cotta for proper drainage.

Some other important thing to remember about watering houseplants:

✔Water in the morning.
✔Use room temperature water .
✔If you're watering every couple of days, you have the wrong soil and drainage.
✔Don't forget the drainage zone created at the bottom of each pot (broken clay, brick, twigs etc.)
✔Avoid watering plants with water from soft water systems. They contain too much sodium.

POTTING MEDIUM & SOIL MIX

The correct potting soil for indoor plants is as important as light and water requirements. The soil should be well-draining, while at the same time able to hold on to enough nutrients and moisture to ensure proper root growth.

Most of the indoor, tropical variety plants come from nurseries that water their plants on a **daily** basis, which means that the soil the nursery uses is extremely porous. The most important thing we can do once we get a new house plant home is to **re-pot it** into a better soil mix.

There are plenty of good pre-mixed, pre-packaged soils available. But you must make sure that such a potting medium has equal amounts of top soil, sand, and humus material. The humus material can be **compost** or it can be **peat moss**. If the bag of potting mix is fluffy and contains no sand or humus material, but a lot of that white styrofoam material, put it back.

If you would rather mix your own soil, all you have to do is combine the equal amounts of sand (builders sand preferably), finely decomposed compost, and top soil. Also incorporate perlite or a permanent soil amendment like *Soil Pro 200* or *Super Dirt*. The permanent soil amendment should amount to, at most, one-fifth of the overall potting medium.

Remember. **Bromeliad** and **flowering plants** require different potting mediums. But, since I promised you **low-maintenance**, stick with the sand/compost/topsoil combo for the basic indoor plants. Such proper potting mediums are also critical when you transplant. If you are doing a good job of growing out the indoor plant, then every few years increase the **pot size** to help the plant from becoming root bound. The obvious first sign your plant needs re-potting is when the roots begin growing out of the container's drainage hole.

FEEDING & FERTILIZING

It doesn't take much to feed indoor plants. Nine times out of ten, all it takes is a twice-a-year feeding of an extremely **slow-release, balanced** fertilizer like a *13-13-13* or *14-14-14*.

When a plant grows outdoors in the ground it is exposed to all kinds of nourishment. But, a potted plant is limited by the soil around it's root system. That's why it's critical to feed the plant twice each year with a slow-release fertilizer. Thus, the **low-maintenance** way.

Caution: There are a large variety of house plant fertilizers and they are sold in many different forms. There's tablets, sticks, liquids, powders, capsules and granules. I suggest the **granular slow-release, balanced fertilizers** twice-a-year; once in the early Spring then once more in the Summer. Balanced, slow-release fertilizers feed your plant for 3-4 four months. Sprinkle the granular form based on plant size on the top of the soil, and when watered in, this provides that slow-release feed for that three to four month period. Do *not* feed it again going into winter, because an actively growing plant is susceptible to damage when cooler weather comes our way.

The most flexible of the feeds, is the **soluble or liquid**. These liquids give you the ability to dilute the amount of feed in order to get just the right amount to a particular plant. That is important because some plants with flowers or different feeding requirements need to be nourished once every two weeks up to once a month. The reason I would avoid sticks or pellets—the ones you shove below the soil line—is because they don't feed as evenly as the sprinkled slow-release granules.

- **Avoid** feeding plants infected with pests or diseases.
- Don't fertilize **dormant** plants.
- Don't **over-fertilize** because leaves are brown or yellow.

Next, here is a list of those plants that I think anyone can grow indoors. Try a couple of these to get your *green thumb* started. Don't go overboard. Just try a couple to start with. The general light requirements for all these indoor plants is plenty of indirect light. No plant can survive without some sort of light be it from indoor lighting or through the windows.

READ THE LABEL for the light requirements given

on the plant when you purchase it. There may be others not on this list that will do well, but this is the list of those plants that do not need specific lighting requirements other than lots of indirect light.

Asparagus Fern
Aspidistra (*Cast Iron Plant*)
Bromeliads
☆Chinese Evergreen☆*Randy's favorite #1*
Croton
Diffenbachia (*Dumb Cane*)
Dracaena (*Cornplant*)
☆Ficus (*Ficus Benjamina*)☆
Every house ought to have one. I've got three.
Norfolk Island Pine
Parlor Palm
☆Philodendron☆*Randy's favorite #2*
Pothos Ivy (*Devil's Ivy*)
Rubber Tree Plant *(Ficus Elastica)*
Schefflera (*Umbrella Tree*)
Snake Plant (*Mother-In-Law Tongue*)
Spathiphyllum (*Peace Lily*)
Spider Plant
☆Synogonium (*Arrowhead Plant*)☆*Randy's favorite #3*
Tolmiea (*Piggyback Plant, & Mother of Thousands*)
Wandering Jew
Wax Plant

Golf Tip #5:

Most new drivers are obsolete before you use them.

Part 9

Insects & Diseases

If it weren't for diseases and insects, gardening would be so simple, right? All we would have to do is water and fertilize. But it's not that easy due in large part to the temperate, humid climate we experience throughout southeast Texas. In fact, insects and plant diseases are battles we must constantly fight. Winters seldom kill our naturalized and hardier varieties of shrubs and trees, but fungal diseases can ravage them. Our intense summers are no match for a well-watered garden, but insects can sure claim an unattended one. This chapter is designed to help you learn what insect pressures and fungal diseases predominate our gardens, and then teach you how to quickly control them . . .

In order to control pests and diseases, you simply cannot ignore your garden. You've got to spend some time there. As *Dr. Sam Cotner*, a long-time horticulturist at Texas A&M, always taught me during my stint at the university, was that the key to successful gardening is keeping your shadow in the garden. What he obviously meant by that, was that an occasional trip amongst the plants, vegetables or flowers always helps.

A neighbor of mine complained that I spent entirely too much time in my front gardens and I was making him look bad, in a sort of peer pressure way. But I considered my occasional walk-through as much a part of my daily routine as checking the mail, feeding the dog, or taking out the trash. When I checked the mail, I pulled a weed. When I fed the dog, I checked for insects, or fungal diseases. When I took out the trash, I pinched back buds to encourage even more flowers. If you only put your shadow in the garden once a week, that's fine, but never allow it to become once a month

Insects can be controlled easily and oftentimes quite naturally if we simply take a look, from time to time, out in the garden. Early infestations of the most problematic insects can be *blown to smithereens* with a simple blast from the garden hose each morning. If we see a pathetic looking part of a plant, and suspect fungal disease, then we hit it then with a fungicide and things are usually back to normal within days. But a fungal disease allowed to linger for more than a month, can eventually kill a plant.

So, now that you're convinced to make an occasional walk-through as much a part of your daily/weekly routines, let's start learning what to be on the lookout for.

INSECTS

APHIDS—Soft, almost oval, pinhead sized insects that huddle together on new growth stems, buds and especially the undersides of leaves. They also come in many colors, from green, to yellow, to pink and brown. Plants affected almost every year by aphids are roses, crape myrtles, camellias, hibiscus and bougainvillea.

Control: Aphids caught early on can easily be blasted off with a burst of water. Heavy infestations can be controlled with repeated sprays of *Insecticidal Soap* if you want to stay in a biological control mode. Also Lacewings, parasitic wasps and small lizards are good natural controls too. Chemically, you can use Chemical controls like *Diazinon, Dursban, Intercept* or *Orthene.*

BORERS—Love both newly planted trees along with weakened or stressed trees. To know that you have borers in Oak trees for example, you would not only look for tiny holes up a few feet and beyond, you will also notice sawdust just on the bark or at the tree's base as a symptom. A heavily infested tree, can die in a matter of days, if the borers are allowed to continue girdling the tree.

Control: Again the only real biological control for borers, is to take better care of the tree, not allowing it to stress. Poor soil, damage limbs and drought weaken a tree enough to invite borers. *Malathion* or *Methoxychlor* (If still available) are the proven Insecticidal sprays for borers.

CATERPILLARS—Worm-like, soft bodied, sometimes hairy, sometimes spiny, almost always green, yellow-green or brown. They have a healthy appetite for foliage, and its choice of plants is wide ranging. But it's a safe bet that when you see a caterpillar and notice other areas of the plant leaves looking as if they've been gnawed upon, then you've got caterpillars.

Control: The best non-chemical control is with Bt, or bacillus thuringiensis, a natural bacteria that is sprayed on foliage. When the caterpillar eats the leaf, it gets sick and dies. You can also control, caterpillars biologically by putting down sharp sand around the base of the plant, or a product with diatomaceous earth. The scratchy substances will damage their soft bodies.

CHINCH BUGS—Tiny black insects with minute white wing pods on each side. They exclusively attack St. Augustine lawns during the hot, dry months. You can rarely see the chinch bug unless you perform a water test to flush them out. That can be done by simply laying a garden hose in one spot and allowing the chinch bug, which hates moisture, to run up on the hose.

Control: The only real biological control is to keep a healthy, well-watered lawn, especially during the hottest summer months. Liquid insecticides like *Diazinon* and *Dursban* have worked well for years, but you must catch the chinch bug early on. Be on the lookout for new insecticides that are being introduced, and read their label for chinch bug control.

CUTWORMS—Are usually the larvae of various night-flying moths, but the surface cutworms are most damaging. They get their appropriate name because they cut off young, tender plants at the ground. Cutworms can affect newly planted annuals and vegetable transplants their foliage and their stems. However, they seldom, if ever, attack hardier evergreen shrubs.

Control: You can control biologically by ringing a collar of cardboard or aluminum foil around new transplants, making sure they're pushed 1" down into the soil. The most effective biological control is with *Bacillus Thuringiensis* (Or a Bt insecticide). Plus, a good layer of mulch also helps keep cutworms at bay. Chemically, you can use liquid *Sevin* or *Diazinon*.

FIRE ANTS—To know them is to hate them. And if you've ever been bitten by one, you know they are aptly named. Fire Ants also tend to be more reddish-brown in color than basic wood or farmer ants. They will pop up seemingly overnight, especially when the soil is loose from a good rain. There is no such thing as an eradication control for fire ants yet.

Control: The two-step method still works best. First, place long-term bait controls like *Amdro* or *Logic* around every mound and scatter over the entire yard. Those are bait formulations that kill over a period of months. Nuisance mounds that pop up can be drenched with liquid insecticides, or treated with powered poisons like *Orthene* for Fire Ants.

LACE BUGS—In Houston especially, if you've got *Azaleas*, you're eventually going to have lace bugs, tiny 1/8" long brown bugs with seemingly transparent, gauze-like wings (hence the name, lace bugs). They suck from the underside of leaves much like aphids do, but they leave a brown almost caramelized excrement. As mentioned they love Azaleas as well as Pyracantha and Garden Mums.

Control: Organic controls are somewhat unusual with lace bugs considering that *Nicotine Sulfate* and well as *Rotenone* have been known to control them. Otherwise, liquid *Sevin, Orthene* and *Malathion* are some of the few specific chemicals that work on lace bugs.

LEAFROLLERS—Also from the caterpillar family, but they tend do their work after rolling themselves within a soft, wide supple leafed plant; for example *Calla Lilies*.

Control: Biological sprays like *Bt (Bacillus Thuringiensis)* works, but it's also important to actually shuck out the rolled up caterpillar. Chemical controls like *Orthene*, and liquid *Sevin* also work to control Leafrollers.

MEALYBUGS—Are oval shaped insects covered with a white, cottony wax. They also tend to cluster in groups and are related to the scale family of insects. However, they multiply rapidly and can deteriorate an indoor plant quickly. Like the scale, mealybugs secrete a honeydew which can make the plant sticky and shiny and eventually become covered with black-sooty mold.

Control: Outdoor plants aren't usually affected by mealybugs, but indoor plants need to be treated biologically with strong sprays of water, or with cotton tip swab treatments of alcohol. Mealybugs can also be controlled by placing indoor plants outdoors on nice days. Chemical treatments on the indoor plants should be kept to pyrethrin-based, or contact killing, insecticides.

SCALE—Since scale insects don't fly and move very little. Few people ever know that they have scale insects. The most insidious scale we see in Texas are tiny little white, hard, waxy shelled insect that sits up and down the middle spine of most leaves and congregates on the stems below. There are some that are brown but they all have the same hard outer shell and secrete honey dew which eventually becomes saturated with a black-sooty mold. The best description I ever heard when a novice was describing a scale infestation, was that it looked like tiny specs of paint someone had spattered all over their holly bushes.

Control: Scale can be controlled quite effectively and biologically with a dormant oil spray, which suffocates the insect. But it must be used when the plant is dormant, or December through February. Otherwise, *Malathion, Intercept, Dursban* or *Diazinon* will also work, but it usually takes more than one application.

SLUGS & SNAILS—Devour entire leaves overnight, but at least we don't have the problems that California has with them (a **slug** is a snail without the shell). They are about 1" long, with slick, slimy, black to greenish-gray bodies. They feed at night devouring leaves and leaving Swiss cheese like holes everywhere.

Control: The first step in controlling slugs and snails is to remove all the dark, dank hiding places they go to during the day. They are also attracted to pans of beer in which they will bloat up and drown. As with caterpillars, diatomaceous earth is another quality biological control, but probably the most popular control is still snail & slug bait. Most of the baits are made with *Metaldehyde.* **Do not** use excessive amounts of salt to kill slugs and snails, because while it does kill the pest, it's bad for the root systems of the plants.

SOUTHERN PINE BARK BEETLE—Are tiny little beetles that are black and no bigger than a grain of rice. The tiny intrusion holes created by pine bark beetles will ooze with sap instead of sawdust. They also only attack pine trees, that have been weakened by physical damage or drought stress or improper drainage. The pitch, or *ooze,* coming from these intrusion holes is usually a yellowish to reddish-white resin mass. Pine needles will turn yellow first, before browning and falling off.

Control: Once a tree is heavily infested, there is little hope of salvage. Prevention is the key to keeping pine bark beetles at bay. If caught early enough, any number of liquid insecticides can be sprayed carefully in the early intrusion holes. If a tree is infected, it must be cut down and hauled away to keep the insect from eventually moving to other trees.

SPIDER MITES—Aren't actually spiders, but **relatives** of spiders. And to the naked eye they look like little dots of red, yellow or black. These itsy-bitsy insects can cause tremendous damage and tend to love *Junipers, Bonsai, Arborvitaes* and perennial flowers like *Lantana*. Although tiny in size they are massive in number and they suck the juice out of evergreen shrubs like a juniper desiccating it leaf by leaf and leaving those leaves mottled and brown or mottled and grayish. To see the mites, hold a piece of white paper under the leaves and tap the leaves. The tiny mites will be visible as black, yellow or red bits of dirt that when looked at up-close, almost look like a spider. Sometimes early in the mornings, a tiny web may be seen thanks to morning dew. And that too is an indication of spider mite infestation.

Control: Miticides are critical in controlling spider mites. Biological controls, outside of spraying the plant down with water, just don't exist. *Kelthane* and *Ethion* are miticides. However some people will spray *Orthene* as a systemic control as well.

THRIPS—Are almost invisible insects that love soft, budding flowers and new leaf tissue as well as emerging fruit. They love rosebuds, hibiscus buds, citrus trees and any number of flowering bushes. Interestingly enough, thrips seem to prefer light to yellow flowers. But they are difficult to eradicate.

Control: The best method to control thrips is to remove any infested leaves, buds or fruit at once. *Malathion* is written to control Thrips, however, it's rather difficult to get an insecticide in contact with these microscopic pests because they infiltrate the many layers of emerging buds.

WHITEFLIES—The *worst* insect in Texas gardens during the 1990's. These sucking insects fit their name perfectly, since they are tiny little versions of flies that have white bodies and white to translucent wings. They will fluff up in the air when you make contact with a branch or large leaf they are on, but they will settle right back down for continuation of their dinner plans. Like aphids and scales whiteflies also secret a honeydew which in turn becomes black-sooty mold on the leaves of plants. They love vegetable gardens to *Crape Myrtles* to every kind of citrus imaginable. They also like a whole host of evergreen shrubs like *Viburnum* and *Ligustrum*.

Control: Biologically, consistent bursts of water sprays each morning can help, but may not totally eradicate the whitefly. I consider alternating controls of contact killers *(Intercept* or *Dursban)* and systemic insecticides *(Orthene)* as the best control for whiteflies. *Malathion* and *Diazinon* are also written for whiteflies, but have become less effective over the years.

Pillbugs, Sowbugs, Earthworms, Stinkbugs (Squash Bugs) **Leaf-Cutter Bees, Leaf-Cutter Ants** and **Earwigs** are all insects that have been known to cause some problems, but only when working in large numbers. Most insecticides mentioned above can also control these insects. But if you're committed to the "shadow-in-the-garden" concept, they will probably never amount to much of a problem. Meanwhile, insects like **leafminers** and **squash vine borers** are found in vegetable gardens and we don't even attempt to tackle vegetable gardens while we should be playing golf.

DISEASES

ANTHRACNOSE—Infects leaves of trees mostly. Anthracnose causes large irregular brown blotches and causes premature dropping of leaves. It can also cause premature twig die-back and canker. The canker is the source for re-infection of Anthracnose the following Spring.

Control: Your first shot at control is to eliminate all sources of future infection. So, prune out all infected limbs and cut out cankers. Then use a fungicide early each spring when leaves are beginning to roll out. *Benomyl, Mancozeb* and *Kocide DF* will work to control Anthracnose.

BLACKSPOT—Is the most common malady of rose growers in Texas, and causes tiny black spots that eventually turn a leaf brown to yellow and they fall off. If black spot is not controlled early, it can defoliate a plant. While it may not kill it right the, a lack of leaves prevents the plant from manufacturing its food effectively. If you're going to have roses where humidity exists, you're going to have black spot.

Control: Experienced rose growers spray all their plants with a fungicide like *Funginex, Benomyl* or *Triforine* every 7-10 days.

It works as both a prevention and a control for existing spots. One way to approach control from an organic perspective is to provide ample aeration around the bushes, ample space between each plant, and trimmed in an open vase form. Remove infected and fallen leaves and throw them away, do not add them to a compost pile.

BROWNPATCH—Circular patches of brown to yellow discoloration of *St. Augustine* turfgrass which usually happens when moisture levels and night time temperatures mix together in a perfect combination. Night time lows will be 60-68° and daytime highs won't exceed 90°, and when there's plenty of moisture from rain, sprinklers or morning dew and fog, expect the fungal spores of brownpatch to grow.

Control: The best control is always a healthy lawn. Provide ample drainage to avoid excess moisture. Also prevent from putting down high nitrogen fertilizers *(See Lawns)*. You can prevent brownpatch with a **systemic fungicide** if you put it out at the right time. That would be one month prior to its yearly emergence. *Bayleton, Benomyl* and *Terraclor* work well. Once it's come up, you must stop it in it's tracks with a **contact fungicide** like *Daconil* or *Terraclor.*

FIRE BLIGHT—Is appropriately named, because when fire blight effects a tree or shrub it gives all the leaves a burned appearance. It's a bacteria that is unfortunately spread by rain, birds and insects. Fruiting trees and ornamental pear trees are especially susceptible.

Control: Once you see an infected branch, prune it off with sterilized pruning sheers. Throw infected leaves and limbs away.

Several applications of fungal sprays have little effect, because remember this is a bacteria, not a fungus. Also avoid high nitrogen fertilizers either for the tree, or on turfgrasses around the tree. The rapid green growth from the nitrogen makes the tree vulnerable as well.

FUNGAL LEAF SPOT—Is related to the black spot fungal disease on roses. Fungal leaf spot is more obvious on evergreen shrubs like *Hawthorns, Ligustrums* and especially *Red Tip Photinias*. It starts as small brown to black spots that turn an entire leaf yellow. The spots can get bigger and defoliate a plant over a period of time. Not necessarily life threatening, but unsightly nonetheless.

Control: One of the best ways to control fungal leaf spot is with an alternating schedule of the fungicides *Daconil* and *Mancozeb. Daconil* helps stop the fungus in it's tracks, while the copper-based *Mancozeb* works as a preventative.

POWDERY MILDEW—Is the bane of most *Crape Myrtle* fans along the Texas Gulf Coast. It is what it says, a white, powdery mold that coats the leaves of roses, *Crape Myrtles,* citrus trees and every sort of *euonymus* plant. The coating of the powdery mildew stunts the growth of the plant and can, if left alone, kill the plant. Plenty of sunshine and air circulation helps keep mildew at bay, but the best thing we can do now is look for resistant varieties of *Crape Myrtles.*

Control: Once is never enough! That is, it takes multiple applications of fungicides to keep powdery mildew under control.

RUST—Remember the old saying,"If it looks like a duck; walks like a duck, and quacks like a duck", it probably **is** a duck . . . ?" Well oftentimes the same can be said for the fungal disease known as rust. If it looks like average rust pustules. (On a leaf of a plant no less), feels like rust and spreads on the fingers like rust, then it probably is rust. Rust affects roses and other flowering plants, but is most notorious on azaleas around Houston. Sadly, while we can do a lot to control rust by gathering up debris and fallen leaves and limbs around affected plants, wind and insects help to spread the fungus too.

Control: Biologically, we can help prevent rust with Sulfur sprays. The fungicides *Funginex* and *Zineb* are also written for rust controls.

Golf Tip#6:

When stock goes down, go out for a round.

Part 10

Calendar Checklist

Golfers, or those who have other fun outside/inside activities you'd rather be doing than gardening, this large list might frighten you because it looks like a lot of work. But, it truly isn't. If it is, gardening is not for you; let someone do it for you.

The fact is, this list is easy and does, in fact, only *look* difficult. It's the **smart way** to make certain your garden and landscape looks superb in the *least* amount of time, with the *least* amount of effort, and for the *least* amount of money.

At the first of each month, or even at the end of the previous month, refer to this list to help jog the memory as to what things can and should be done. By staying current with the list, you've done everything at the first of the month and you will allow time for the things you truly like to do. Remember, I said I would make it *easier* for you, not eliminate the work completely.

GGG Garden Checklist for January

BEST TIP OF THE MONTH: Plant *Tulip* bulbs or any other unplanted bulbs.

Plant a tree on Arbor Day, the third Friday in January. Trees are permanent and easy to care for.

Prune established trees while in the dormancy state.

Prepare soil areas for those vegetable and flower gardens later in the Spring.

Check *Junipers* and other narrowleaf evergreens for bagworm pouches.

Extend the life of potted Christmas plants (Poinsettia) by keeping the soil moist and away from warm air (60°-65° is best).

Feed cool-season annuals, like *Pansies,* a light application of blooming plant food.

Fertilize established trees and shrubs with a *balanced, slow-release* fertilizer.

If you are interested in planting a vegetable garden, my co-host on GardenLine, John Burrow, has an excellent book out titled, **VEGETABLE GARDENING *SPRING & FALL.***

Scale insects can be controlled biologicailly during winter months with a dormant oil spray.

Prune fruit and nut trees, removing all dead and damaged limbs. Then leave outer most limbs intact for easy harvest access.

Take in mowers, trimmers, and blowers for maintenance or needed repairs. Do it now before eveyone else does this spring.

GGG Garden Checklist for February

BEST TIP OF THE MONTH: To avoid grassy weeds later in the spring and summer, apply pre-emergent herbicides for grassy weeds **NOW!** Repeat the application 90 days later.

BETTER TIP OF THE MONTH: Begin thinking about pruning back twiggy growth and shaping your Crape Myrtle. Make sure all expired seed pods are pruned as well to insure better bloom production.

Apply *broadleaf weed killers* on warm days for early control.

Prune back roses no shorter than 18", but preferably 50% of all canes. Make all cuts ½ to ¼" above outward facing buds. **DO NOT PRUNE** climbing roses, or those considered one-time bloomers.

Perfect time to prune peach and plum trees.

Apply horticultural oil sprays to scale-prone plants before they become a problem.

Azaleas lose some leaves in early February so they can make room for new leaves.

DO NOT PRUNE blooming trees and shrubs or you will be cutting off the blooming wood.

Fertilize trees and shrubs (except Azaleas, Camellias and Gardenias) with a balanced slow-release fertilizer.

Trim groundcover now so they will spread faster through the rest of the spring.

Attend **Home & Garden** shows for new ideas.

Prune back lanky *Nandinas*. By taking off the top third of the longest canes they will fill in from below.

If you've got pecan trees, feed them now!

Mow for the first time and "scalp" the lawn.

DO NOT USE "weed & feed" products on SE Texas lawns.

Use a soil activator on the lawn to enhance microbial activity in the soil.

Still a good month to transplant any containerized trees or shrubs.

Good month for planting easy-to-grow strawberries.

GGG Garden Checklist for March

GGG BEST TIP OF THE MONTH: Feed Azalea and Camellia plants once they finish blooming, then again in 6 weeks. Fertilize **ROSES** once every month from now until the end of September.

Prune back spring-flowering shrubs, like Azaleas—once the blooming cycle is finished.

Good time to replace or replenish mulching material in flower beds and shrub borders.

Begin your roses on a weekly regiment with a fungicide to control black spot and powdery mildew.

Although vegetable gardens are high maintenance chores, **tomato, pepper and squash** plants are the *easiest* of all vegetables to grow.

Beware of close-out sales on bare-root trees and shrubs. Their chance of survival is limited this late in the season. Depend on **containerized** trees and shrubs at this time of the year.

"Scalp" your lawn (if you didn't do so in late February). This removes winter stubble and opens the roots to sunshine and oxygen.

Remove any dead or damaged limbs, or freeze damaged limbs from trees and shrubs.

If you've got pecans, and didn't feed them in February, do so now.

Be on the lookout for *pillbug* and *sowbug* infestations. Use a pillbug/sowbug bait or **Sevin Dust** onto the surrounding foliage and soil.

You can control caterpillars that are eating tender foliage plants with an insecticide that kills off only worms and caterpillars.

Prune and feed climbing roses.

Pinch back established perennials when they set their first sprouts.

March is the best time to visit gardening shows from all the "Societies".

Buy lawn fertilizer for April feeding.

GGG Garden Checklist for April

GGG BEST TIP OF THE MONTH: Apply your 3-1-2 ratio lawn fertilizer during the first week of April. **DO NOT USE** "weed & feed" formulations.

Prune back spring flowering shrubs and feed with acid type fertilizer.

Continue to spray roses to control black spot with fungicide.

When selecting annual transplants, look for short, compact plants.

The best time to find uncommon plants. Nursery stock is always at it's best selection during the month of April.

Plant spring annuals now.

The best month for re-potting overgrown houseplants.

Move your mower to it's highest setting from now on.

Yellowing leaves on the new growth of many plants indicates iron chlorosis. Use **iron/sulfur additives** to correct the problems.

Be on the lookout for **aphid** insects. They will attack plants with ample tender, new growth.

To help control fleas, insecticides like *Dursban* and *Diazinon* can be used outdoors.

Outdoor tropical plants, like Hibiscus and Bougainvillaeas need **tropical plant foods**.

Most all flower and shrubs do best in beds that have been raised a minimum of 6-8 above the soil line.

Time to plant perennials.

Although Bluebonnets look beautiful on the roadsides, they are best planted by seed in the fall.

Good month to plant Caladium bulbs, since the soil temperature is finally above 70°.

If you must plant tomato plants, choose large plants because it might be too hot for good growth.

GGG Garden Checklist for May

BEST TIP OF THE MONTH: Remember to **replace or replenish mulch**

material in flower beds and shrub borders.

Remove old blossoms of spring annuals like **Pansies, Calendulas, Stock** and **Snapdragons** to encourage a longer flowering season.

Continue to fertilize **roses** with small amounts of high nitrogen fertilizers once a month until the end of September. And Spray weekly to control **black spot** and **powdery mildew**.

Start looking for **powdery mildew** on your Crape Myrtles. Fungicides like *Consan* will wash the mildew off with at least two applications.

Plant *Impatiens, Pentas* and *Caladiums* in shady areas.

Final cuts on freeze-damaged trees and shrubs can finally be made. Remove all dead wood until you see green in the cambium layer.

If you haven't yet fertilized, apply a *3-1-2* ratio slow-release formula.

Be on the lookout our for disease (leaf spot) on Photinias, Hawthorns and Ligustrums. Use fungicide like *Mancozeb* or *Maneb* with *Daconil.*

Also be on the lookout for **early blight** in tomatoes, which cause large yellow and browning leaf blotches. Again control with *Daconil* fungicide.

Make second application of pre-emergent grassy weed killer to **prevent** *Crabgrass* and *Grassburs.*

Nutgrass and Virginia Buttonweed can be controlled with an herbicide.

Feed *Crape Myrtles* and summer-blooming shrubs with **high phosphorous** (high middle number) fertilizers.

For bigger, better Caladiums, feed them **blood meal**.

Plant **Oleanders** since they are hardy in conditions of total sun.

Don't forget Mother's Day! In fact, buy her a plant.

Plant warmer season annuals such as *Purslane, Moss Rose* and *Vincas.*

GGG Gardening Checklist for June

BEST TIP OF THE MONTH: Develop good irrigation practices by June for your lawn. As a general rule, *St. Augustine* lawns need **one full inch** of water per week. If it hasn't rained that much, supplement the irrigation.

If you don't **already** have some *Hibiscus,* this is a good month to plant new ones.

Remember to **feed** tropical flowering plants like *Bougainvillaeas* and *Hibiscus* with tropical plant foods (those specifically designed for Hibiscus.)

Make critical notes of your landscape during these hot summer months. What needs more water than normal? What grows too fast? How can it be rearranged, etc?

Spider mites can become a big problem on **conifers** and **perennials** like *Lantana* during this time of the year. They are best controlled with a **systemic miticide**. Also look for miticides like *Kelthane* for contact kill.

The best time to water **turfgrasses** is early in the morning. And, try **never** to water between 2pm to 6pm. There's too much evaporation because of the heat, and watering at that time also invites diseases/fungal stresses.

Most wood mulches should be applied and kept at a depth of **two inches**. However, the courser the material the deeper the mulch should be. Two inches of **shredded hard wood mulch** has the same effect as **4 inches** of *Coastal Bermuda Hay.*

Use iron/sulfur additives to correct yellowing or chlorosis (indicated by yellowing leaves with dark green veins.) Prominate in acid loving plants like azaleas and gardenias.

Be on the lookout for fungal leaf spots on photinias, hawthorns and ligustrums. Control with alternating fungecides Mancozeb and Daconil.

GGG Gardening Checklist for July

BEST TIP OF THE MONTH: Looking for a new annual that is different in size, shape and color? Look for **Copper plants**. July 1st is the best time to plant them.

Are you keeping up with a consistent watering regimen? Irrigation systems should run **early** in the morning.

First week of July is time for our **second application** of premium *3-1-2 (15-5-10)* ratio lawn food. Remember to stay away from "weed and feed" combinations.

If you're interested in a **fall vegetable garden**, start preparing the bed now with equal amounts of top soil, composted humus and sharp sand.

If you've got **fruit trees**, feed them **now** that they've finished producing. They require high nitrogen fertilizers designed for fruit tree production.

Roses could use a light pruning to keep them in check and vibrant.

July is the month we should clip off dead and dying seed pods on *Crape Myrtles*. This will encourage a whole new set of blooms from August till the first frost.

Black Sooty Mold on any green plant usually indicates *aphids, scale* or *white flies*. These insects can be controlled with an alternating treatment of a **systemic insecticide** like *Orthene,* and a contact killer such as *Dursban* or any *pyrethrin.*

Caladiums require plenty of water at this time of the year. They also respond to a **nitrogen only** fertilization.

Evergreen plants with berries will show drought stress by dropping berries. Don't forget to water them as well.

Hold off on any major pruning from now until January for shrubs and trees. Light pruning of shrubs like *Photinias* is acceptable.

If you like bulbs, this is the time to make your selection of **spring flowering bulbs** that are to be planted in October and November.

GGG Gardening Checklist for August

BEST TIP OF THE MONTH: Prune off all Crape Myrtle seed heads. It will help encourage some new blooms for the fall.

Begin establishment of **compost pile** NOW, to accommodate fall leaf drop. (My co-host on GardenLine, John Burrow, has **all** about building a compost bin in his first book, YOUR FRONT YARD)

Remember to **pick off flowers now**, and (again) on most annuals to encourage even more flower production.

It is not too late to set out another planting of warm season annuals such as **Celosia, Zinnias, Vinca**, and **Marigolds**. They will require extra water for the first two weeks, but they should reward you with great color through the fall.

If you have *Cannas*, be on the lookout for **leafroller insects**. They will literally and physically roll the broad leaf up and start sucking the life from each individual plant. Use a *systemic insecticide* of physically **shuck** the worm from the rolled up leaf.

Good time to control *Nutsedge* and *Virginia Buttonweed* with a **selective herbicide** like *Image*. When it gets above 96°, *Image* will not work.

Continue to watch for **fungal leaf spots** on *Photinias* and *Hawthorns,* and control with **Daconil** and **Mancozeb**.

BETTER TIP OF THE MONTH: Prune hybrid Tea Roses by ¼" to ⅓", to reshape for fall blooms.

Fall webworms in pecan trees can be controlled with Bacillus thuringiensis Bt.

GGG Gardening Checklist for September

BEST TIP ON THE MONTH: Look for the advent of **Bulb Marts**, especially in larger cities like Houston. Houston's has always been towards the latter part of September. Buy some for refrigeration now like *Tulips* and *Hyacinths*. Plant others now like Lilies and *Irisis*.

Big month for planting easy-to-grow vegetables such as tomatoes and peppers; don't wait until the end of the month. They must be protected, however, from potential intense Summer temperatures.

Wanna try **wildflower seeds** for next spring? Plant them now and make sure each seed makes firm contact with dirt for germination success.

Good month to plant *Chrysanthemums* from pots to the landscape; they give you immediate color. Fertilize them once every two weeks with blooming plant foods.

Be prepared to apply **pre-emergent herbicides** to help control **broadleaf weeds** the are a nuisance in January.

If you are finding more than **4 grub worms** per square inch just beneath the turfgrass, you've probably got an infestation that needs control. *Liquid Dursban or Intercept* works best to control grubworm damage.

If **Brownpatch** was more of a problem late October into November last year, put down a **systemic fungicide** with *Bayleton* or *Terraclor* immediately! If Brownpatch **circles** are starting already, use *Daconil* fungicide to stop it in its tracks. Make two applications 7-10 days apart.

Establish **compost pile** for fall leaf accumulation.

If you see **whitefly infestations** on flowering shrubs like *Hibiscus* and *Crape Myrtles*, you can interrupt their cycle naturally by **blasting off** all you see early each morning with a high pressure spray of water.

Despite the show of *Pansies* at many nurseries in September, **don't plant them** until late October early November in SE Texas.

GGG Gardening Checklist for October

GGG BEST TIP OF THE MONTH: *Apply pre-emergent herbicides* to your **turfgrasses** now, to control **broadleaf weeds** that are a nuisance in the winter months.

October is the perfect month to **transplant shrubs, trees and perennials.** Get them established now and they will reward you with good growth in the spring.

Begin planting spring flowering bulbs. General rule of thumb: Plant bulbs as deep as their size. Example—a 2" bulb needs to be **two inches** below the soil line. Except for *Tulips* and Hyacinths, have all bulbs planted by the end of the month.

BETTER TIP OF THE MONTH: **Winterize your lawn** with a winterizing formulated fertilizer. Good examples would be *18-6-12.* The key number is the third one, *12,* which is **Potassium** and a key for good root growth during the winter months.

You can **stop feeding roses** on a monthly basis, but do water.

Tropical plants like *Hibiscus* **need a good layer of mulch** to protect them going in to winter.

If you have *Caladiums,* dig them up by the end of the month. Store the tubers in a cool, dry place over the winter.

It's a good time to **divide and transplant overcrowded perennials**, as well as *Daylillies* and *Narcissus*.

If you like 10-15 onions, **plant the seeds in October**. That's where they got their name, **10-15**, it was the optimum planting date years ago.

Stay on the look for fungal diseases in turfgrasses. Brownpatch can be prevented with a **systemic lawn fungicide** with *Bayleton* or *Benomyl.* If it's already showing, apply a contact fungicide to stop further spread. *Daconil* or *Terraclor* works well in such a case.

Be on the lookout for **grubworms** in the lawn. If you find more than 4-5 per square foot, treat with an liquid insecticide like **Dursban.**

GGG Gardening Checklist for November

BEST TIP OF THE MONTH: Plant your Pansies and other cool-season annuals NOW! Incorporate a pansy food to the soil before planting like *Color Star* or *Easy Gro Pansy and Blooming Plant Food.*

Broadleaf weeds that have popped up, **must** be controlled with a **post-emergent herbicide**. Look for a broad-leafed weed killer. There are many on the market, but most are based on the 2-4D formulation. (**Ortho's** *Weed-B-Gone,* and **Greenlight's** *Wipe Out)*

Cyclamens add cool season color to areas that are mostly shaded.

If you know a freeze is on the way, water in-ground plants. A dry root zone is more susceptible to freeze damage.

Give gardening gifts to the "green thumbs" in your family; pH meters, hand trowel kits, bird feeders and gardening books from seeds to trees always make good gifts.

Perfect time of the year to have your soil tested by the Extension Service. Then you'll know exactly what kind of fertilizer you should or shouldn't be using in the spring. Most full-service nurseries have soil-test kits available. Otherwise contact your **County Extension Office**. (Call *information* and ask for the one in your area.)

Falling leaves and needles make great mulches for compost pile material. Do not bag them for the landfill.

Cut banana stalks back to six feet or less. Prepare to wrap them during freezes with burlap or carpet remnants.

GGG Gardening Checklist for December

BEST TIP OF THE MONTH: Find the closest **Christmas Tree Farm** (or choose-and-cut operation) for your Christmas tree this year. Texas-grown trees are fresher and it's a wonderful family experience.

If you haven't applied a new layer of mulch to your beds in November, do it **NOW!** This will help conserve moisture and protect root systems from freezes.

Be on the lookout for scale insects (look like specs of white paint up and down the leaves). Scales love *hollies, camellia, euonymus, privets, hawthorns* and *photinias.* **Use a horticultural oil/dormant oil.** This suffocates the insect. If above 70°, use an insecticide.

If there is little rain during the month, don't forget to water both plants and turf. Soak them both deeply because even though there is little top growth the roots are still very active.

You can do minor pruning of trees and shrubs, but the major pruning should be left until winter when they are in their highest state of dormancy.

Don't forget that there are many more cool-season annual options other than pansies. Look for *English Daisies, Calendulas, Sweet Alyssum, Stocks, Pinks, Snapdragons* and *Ornamental Kale* and *Cabbage.*

If you don't have a compost pile, start one with all the leaves, pine needles and yard waste you collect during the fall and winter.

Since banana plants are popular in these parts, remember to **cut them back to a manageable height** of 4, 5 or 6 feet so you can wrap the stock during freezing spells.

Golf Tip #7:

Golf putting is like life: Too short and not hard enough.

ABOUT THE AUTHOR

Born in Whittier, California in 1962, Randy's family moved to Houston when he was five. His father was a Mechanical Engineer and his mom, a housewife. Randy's mom loved gardening and took a lot of pride in the uniqueness of her back yard. Her wish was that everyone who visited felt they were in a Better Homes & Garden setting. One sister, Terri, is married and lives in Pearland.

Randy attended Robert E. Lee high school in Houston and Texas A&M University where he received his first degree in Broadcast Journalism. He returned to A & M to work for the College of Agriculture and Life Sciences to produce radio and television material, where he also garnered his Masters degree in Agriculture.

Part of his job was a spokesperson for the college where he researched and disseminated information on topics like *Africanized Honey Bees* and *Red Imported Fire Ants.* He also produced radio and television pieces on-everything from beef cattle to horiculture.

In 1986 He worked with Bill Zak and Ben Oldag, who then had the KTRH garden show. When Bill Zak retired in December of 1995, John Burrow suggested Randy as a replacement. Now, he and John have formed a new, exciting team. Judging from ratings and the number of advertisers, they are doing an exceptional job.

This book, Randy's first full-length book, takes you step by step, through almost **each** day of **each** month of the year. It is **easy** to read, and the instructions are **easy** to follow. It truly **is,** a **GOLFER'S GUIDE TO GARDENING!**

Pete Billac
Editor/Publisher

Other Books by Swan Publishing

ALL ABOUT TREES IN & AROUND HOUSTON—Tree expert, John Foster, tells everything you need to know about selecting the best trees, planting, pruning, fertilizing, diagnosing diseases, root barriers & more . . . . $ 9.95

BOOKS BY TOM TYNAN:

Volume 1. Home Improvement *Homeowner's most often asked questions*—Saves you thousands of dollars on easy-to repair items in your home that **you** can do! . . . . $ 9.95

Volume 2. Building and Remodeling—How to setup for a large job. Whether you should do it or have it done. How to choose a contractor, subs, get a loan, call an inspection, get permits, insurance, architects, etc. . . . . $ 9.95

Volume 3. Buying & Selling A Home—A book used by many Realtors. Secrets on selling and on buying. What to fix and, what **not** to fix. What to paint. What to clean. Where to get the greatest return on your dollar. A **great** book! . . . . $ 9.95

Volume 4. Step by Step 15 Energy-Saving Projects—Simple, inexpensive projects for your home that will save you money on your energy bills . . . . $ 9.95

BOOKS BY JOHN BURROW:

Your Front Yard—Everything you need to know about growing healthy grass, shrubs and flowers. A book with answers most homeowners are afraid to ask. A quick reference guide. . .$ 9.95

Vegetable Gardening *Spring & Fall*—What to grow and when to grow it; in city, country, even patio gardens. Vegetables from A to Z. The vegetable book planting guide for Texas . . $ 9.95

RANDY LEMMON is available for personal appearances, luncheons, banquets, seminars, etc. Call (281) 388-2547 for cost and availability.

★ ★ ★ ★ ★

For each book, send a personal check or money order in the amount of $12.85 per copy to:
Swan Publishing, 126 Live Oak, Alvin, TX, 77511.

★ ★ ★ ★ ★

LIBRARIES—BOOKSTORES—QUANTITY ORDERS

Swan Publishing
126 Live Oak
Alvin, TX 77511

To order by major credit card 24 hours a day call:
(281) 268-6776 or long distance 1-800-866-8962
Fax: (281) 585-3738

Delivery in 2-7 days